The book of Job documents a godly man wrestling for truth in the midst of his suffering. Lauri Hogle's new book takes readers through Job's story and beyond that, to the life of Christ who suffered in our place, pointing us to our eternal hope in Him. Throughout the book, readers are challenged to confront lies with the truth of the gospel. For all those who suffer, Lauri is a fitting guide, leading hurting hearts to Jesus.

CHRISTINA FOX, SPEAKER & AUTHOR

Lauri Hogle's book ministered to my soul as she applied a robust understanding of God's sovereignty in difficult providences to the practical struggles of life. Lauri does an excellent job communicating the hard truths of the book of Job, and how God uses His people's suffering for their good and His glory. Her personal story helps make difficult truth simple to understand and will be a balm for the souls of weary sufferers.

REV. JEREMY BYRD, PASTOR
CHRIST CHURCH ANN ARBOR, MI (PCA)

This book is amazing! I consider it a must-read for those who are going through extended suffering or caring for those who are. You'll find HOPE and ENCOURAGEMENT as you renew your mind in the truths Lauri shares.

I found her illustrations very transparent making them very powerful as she shared her story—her struggles—her agony—her walk with the Lord and His loyal love for her! To God be the glory!!!!

I love the "lies" verses "truths" laid out in such a helpful way. Excellent! It is my view that everything throughout this book is "rightly divided" and I believe Lauri is a "worker who need not be ashamed." Lauri gets my "Excellence award," but my "well done" ultimately doesn't count.

It is my pastoral and personal view she has been used of the Lord in this book to clearly communicate His Word, in a practical way that will be used by Him to help many others for years, even generations to come.

And in that, along with a lifetime of faithfulness, I'm confident she will hear "well done."

You need to read this book as I believe it will become a classic for those who suffer and those who counsel and care for those who are suffering.

LARRY G. BRODIE, EXECUTIVE PASTOR
TIMBERLAKE BAPTIST CHURCH, LYNCHBURG, VA

How have Christians through the ages responded to suffering and trials in life? By standing on the truths of God's word and reminding themselves of those truths no matter how difficult circumstances become.

Born from her own circumstances, Lauri Hogle uses the narrative of Job to point Christians to the only true hope we have when we suffer in life —the living Word of God. Then, in each chapter, she challenges us to sing those truths to ourselves through classic hymns of the Christian faith.

This devotional book could only come from someone who has already walked this road, and it speaks to fellow sufferers to find their hope in the One who has come to make all things new!

KEVIN STRINGHAM
FAMILY & DISCIPLESHIP PASTOR, STAFF ELDER
FOUNTAIN CHURCH, LAGRANGE, GA

Lauri, with raw honesty, tackles the painful questions that arise in our hearts when suffering is our constant companion. By massaging the truth of God's Word into our hearts, she brings us to Jesus. This book reminds us that our Savior walks alongside us in our suffering and offers us hope and joy even in the midst of our pain. The structure and the riches of this book are a valuable resource to women as we journey home.

JUDIE PUCKETT, DIRECTOR OF WOMEN'S MINISTRIES
CHAPELGATE PRESBYTERIAN CHURCH, MARRIOTTSVILLE,
MD (PCA)

My friend Lauri knows the story of suffering. But more importantly, she knows the suffering Christ, and she knows Him intimately. In this easily readable devotional, Lauri invites us to journey with Job. She names the lies we are tempted to believe in stories of suffering and the truths of Scripture that we need to recall. If you or someone you know walks the path of suffering, take up this book as a kind gift of gospel rest and hope.

ELIZABETH REYNOLDS TURNAGE
BIBLE TEACHER & GOSPEL COACH
AUTHOR OF:
THE WAITING ROOM & *FROM RECOVERY TO RESTORATION*

When suffering comes our way in life, in all of its varied forms, we often don't know what to do with it. It's a real test of faith: we ask questions that we've never asked before, feel emotions that are new to us, and desperately look for someone who understands what we are going through.

Lauri Hogle has walked the road of suffering in her own life, and like the apostle Paul before her (2 Corinthians 1), longs to share how God has helped her in the midst of it, that her comfort might be yours as well.

If you are suffering today, in this book you'll find an author familiar with some of the deep questions of your heart and mind, and someone who constantly points you back to the Good News of Jesus Christ and the truth of His Word.

As Lauri writes, if no one else understands what you are going through, "Our triune God understands...so our suffering can become a deepened time of intimate fellowship with Him, of abiding in Him, [and] seeking to hear His voice speak back to our cries through His Word."

DAN SOUTHAM, LEAD PASTOR
PARKSIDE HEIGHTS CHURCH, OH

SINGING THE GOSPEL TO JOB

FINDING HOPE IN SUFFERING

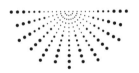

LAURI A. HOGLE, PHD

Trade paperback ISBN: 979-8-9855573-2-9
ePub ISBN: 979-8-9855573-3-6

❀ Created with Vellum

CONTENTS

"THIS IS MY STORY, THIS IS MY SONG!"

It was the moment I'd been waiting for. A mother at 25. I cradled my baby, comforted her cries, sang to her, enchanted by her. My joy over-flowed into loving baby and husband and music work. Two months later, the pain began. I started dropping things.

SO tired.

Like the flu.

All the time.

Multiple doctors ran every test. No diagnosis. "Maybe you're depressed. You're a hypochondriac. We don't have any answers for you."

I delightfully served Jesus Christ as a church music director, organist, pianist, and choral director. I taught children's choirs, piano, voice, and organ. I worked as a music therapist. I often wrote in prayer journals as I studied my Bible. But my prayers became pleas for the mundane:

God give me strength for laundry today. It's so hard to carry it when I hurt so much...OK, I'll take a warm bath to soothe the aches. I can rest the remainder of the day away and serve leftovers.

"I am not at ease, nor am I quiet. I have no rest, but trouble comes" (Job 3:26).

God graciously reminded me of His loving presence, by His Spirit's illumination of Scripture. Call and response prayer included hymns I'd cherished playing, singing, and teaching.

♪♪♪

O the deep, deep love of Jesus!
Love of ev'ry love the best:
'tis an ocean vast of blessing,
'tis a haven sweet of rest.

("O THE DEEP, DEEP LOVE OF JESUS," FRANCIS, S. T., C. 1890)

♪♪♪

Lord, I'm clinging to Your love. I praise you and I love you. Thank you for holding me tight through the pain as I try to hold my baby.

"Can a woman forget her nursing child, that she should have no compassion on the son of her womb? Even these may forget, yet I will not forget you" (Isaiah 49:15).

He comforted me with His mercy and compassion, reminding me that Jesus Himself knows my pain intimately.

"Sing for joy, O heavens, and exult, O earth; break forth, O mountains, into singing! For the LORD has comforted His people and will have compassion on His afflicted" (Isaiah 49:13).

Lord, I take comfort in Your words. I am inscribed on the palms of Your hands (Isaiah 49:16).

♪♪♪

Every day the Lord himself is near me
with a special mercy for each hour;

All my cares he fain would bear, and cheer me,
He whose name is Counselor and Power.
The protection of his child and treasure
Is a charge that on himself he laid;
"As your days, your strength shall be in measure,"
This the pledge to me he made.

("DAY BY DAY AND WITH EACH PASSING MOMENT," SANDELL, C., 1865)

♪♪♪

Then, steroids helped! Baby twin girls arrived, and I again taught choirs, sang, and played organ and piano. But symptoms soon expanded with violent, never-ending headaches, trouble standing up, fuzzy mind, passing out, ambulances, hospitals, medications that didn't help, and valiant rescue attempts.

The Lord provided daily protection and faith as my physical condition worsened.

Father, I'm slogging through this afternoon in pain and weakness. Fill me with Your patience and Your joy. Help me to treat the girls as Jesus would. Help me to praise You and sing for joy.

"But you, O LORD, are a shield about me,
my glory, and the lifter of my head" (Psalm 3:3).

"In peace I will both lie down and sleep;
for you alone, O LORD, make me dwell in safety" (Psalm 4:8).

"But let all who take refuge in you rejoice;
let them ever sing for joy,
and spread your protection over them,
that those who love your name may exult in you" (Psalm 5:11).

As in Psalms of lament, He turned my heart to praise amidst challenges and transitions:

"The LORD is my strength and my shield; in him my heart

trusts, and I am helped; my heart exults, and with my song will I give thanks to him" (Psalm 28:7).

≈

Baltimore recruited my husband for a job, near my family. His work friend immediately connected us with Johns Hopkins Hospital. As our daughters entered school, multiple organ systems began to become dysfunctional. I identified with Job's words as my severe, still-undiagnosed illness worsened:

Bedridden
Hospital
Continual church meal trains

Prayers
Lament
Grief

Surrender to Him

I relinquished dreams of a clean house, little girls dressed in crisp dresses with braided hair, cooking nutritious meals for my family, and energetically supporting my husband. My musical sharing was silenced. I grieved the loss of identity, control, and ability to plan anything. Doctors gave me no hope for restored health as medical tests offered no answers.

Before illness, I ran as an overachieving, workaholic, in-control Christian woman. I had loved and served Jesus, but disease produced deepening dependence on Him for every moment. He cocooned me into a listening place.

Help me, Father. How can I do the housework? I hurt so bad, and I'm so tired. Help me.

≈

ANSWERED PRAYER FOR HELP: KEEP SINGING PRAISE...
AND TRUST GOD

"My heart is steadfast, O God! I will sing and make melody with all my being! I will give thanks to you, O LORD, among the peoples; I will sing praises to you among the nations.

For your steadfast love is great above the heavens; your faithfulness reaches to the clouds.

Be exalted, O God, above the heavens! Let your glory be over all the earth!" (Psalm 108:1, 3-5)

Lord, You are teaching me to praise and trust You. "My heart is steadfast, O God...I will sing and make melody!"(Psalm 57:7)

"For Your steadfast love is great to the heavens, Your faithfulness to the clouds" (Psalm 57:10).

♪♪♪

Great is Thy faithfulness
Morning by morning, new mercies I see.
All I have needed, Thy hand hath provided.
Great is Thy faithfulness, Lord, unto me.

("GREAT IS THY FAITHFULNESS," CHISHOLM, T. O., 1923)

♪♪♪

PRAISE INTERRUPTIONS

So patiently, God taught me who He is and how deeply He loved me as I wrestled with "why?" and constantly cried, "please fix this." He graciously provided a continual way to cognitively, emotionally, and physically battle. He showed me how to endure each day by weakly singing to Him with *praise interruptions.*

Singing praise to God fostered trust in God.

Healing and tearful cleansing materialized as He bathed me in Scripture and song during personal worship moments. As He illuminated Himself in His Word, He continually produced joy, peace, hope, and contentment that replaced my depressive, anxious and frustrated thoughts.

Eternal life, through Jesus Christ, was my comfort and hope.

Oh Lord, You are mighty and holy and amazing and marvelous! I praise Your holy name and worship You! I can't wait to see You and to be with You forever! How great Thou art!

♪♪♪

Lifted up was he to die,
"It is finished!" was his cry;
Now in heav'n exalted high:
Hallelujah! what a Savior!

("Man of Sorrows! What a Name," Bliss, P., 1875)

♪♪♪

I CAN'T. GOD CAN.

Oh Father, I can't do it today without You. I'm sore, tired, grumpy. Demands, cleaning, children, laundry...it's all bearing down on me. Give me the strength to do what's necessary. Help me to love. I'm afraid of this fatigue and the headaches.

"It is the LORD who goes before you; He will be with you; he will not leave you or forsake you" (Deuteronomy 31:8).

"Casting all your anxieties on him, because he cares for you" (1 Peter 5:7), "be still, and know that I am God. I will be exalted among the nations, I will be exalted in the earth!" (Psalm 46:10).

*Eternal God, praising You with music is a powerful weapon You've given
me in this battle. Help me sing to take my thoughts captive to obey Christ
(2 Corinthians 10:5). Give me Your victory over the enemy's attacks.
Renew my mind (Romans 12:2) as I sing of You. Emotional strength. Joy
as I suffer. No self-pity. Teach me more of Your peace and love so I can
endure. Use this to make me more like Christ. As my body fails, please give
me Your inner shalom.*

**"Whom have I in heaven but you? And there is nothing on earth
that I desire besides you. My flesh and my heart may fail, but God
is the strength of my heart and my portion forever" (Psalm
73:25-26).**

**"My peace I give to you...Let not your hearts be troubled, neither
let them be afraid" (John 14:27).**

♪♪♪

*How firm a foundation,
you saints of the Lord.
"Fear not, I am with you,
O be not dismayed;
for I am your God, and will still give you aid;
I'll strengthen you, help you,
and cause you to stand,
upheld by my righteous, omnipotent hand."*

(How Firm A Foundation," K., 1787)

♪♪♪

*Jesus. Exhaustion. Inability to care for the kids. I'm feeling so down. My
body is breaking down. I praise You for giving me the endurance that ends
in joy.*

**"For we know that if the tent that is our earthly home is
destroyed, we have a building from God, a house not made with
hands, eternal in the heavens. For in this tent we groan, longing
to put on our heavenly dwelling" (2 Corinthians 5:1-2).**

"So we do not lose heart. Though our outer self is wasting away, our inner self is being renewed day by day" (2 Corinthians 4:16).

PRAISING PRODUCED REST IN GOD'S SOVEREIGN CARE

Oh Lord, our Lord, how majestic is Your name in all the earth! You are so awesome, so powerful, and all-knowing! Thank you for the rain, the birds, sleep, toys, and supportive friends to run errands. Continue Your work in me. With all these meds, please make this body whole physically. Help me to be patient. You know the right drug, the proper treatment, the whole story. You are the sovereign One who reigns, bringing about Your perfect purpose and plan.

"Declaring the end from the beginning and from ancient times things not yet done, saying, 'My counsel shall stand, and I will accomplish all my purpose'"(Isaiah 46:10).

"Where were you when I laid the foundation of the earth? Who determined its measurements...Have you commanded the morning since your days began, and caused the dawn to know its place...Can you lift up your voice to the clouds, that a flood of waters may cover you?" (Job 38:4, 5, 12, 34)

Sovereign and reigning Lord, show me how to pray. We are so scared. We need You, Your perfect guidance and wisdom. I know You can make anything happen by Your power.

∼

"Satisfy us in the morning with your steadfast love, that we may rejoice and be glad all our days" (Psalm 90:14).

I just want to cry. I can hardly sit with You. I can't read Your Word or write anymore. I can't think. I keep going blind. I keep losing consciousness. I need Your power over my illness.

Take it over so I can sustain any tasks and life You will for me, for Your glory. Help me to be satisfied, rejoicing in all things.

♪♪♪

Be still, my soul:
Your God will undertake to guide the future as he has the past.
Your hope, your confidence let nothing shake;
All now mysterious shall be bright at last.

("BE STILL, MY SOUL," VON SCHLEGEL, K.,1752)

♪♪♪

"It is good to give thanks to the LORD,
to sing praises to your name, O Most High;
to declare your steadfast love in the morning,
and your faithfulness by night.
How great are your works, O LORD!
Your thoughts are very deep!" (Psalm 92:1-2, 5)

Mighty God, You control all. Moments that seem all-wrong are in Your
all-loving plan for me. For Thine is the kingdom and the power and the
glory forever! Satan is subject to Your perfect purposes. You are KING. In
Jesus' matchless name, amen.

♪♪♪

Rejoice, the Lord is King!
Jesus, the Savior reigns, the God of truth and love...
His kingdom cannot fail, he rules o'er earth and heav'n...
He sits at God's right hand till all his foes submit...

("REJOICE, THE LORD IS KING," WESLEY, C., 1746)

♪♪♪

Father, I count on You as a shield around me. You are my strong shelter.
How small I am. How big You are.

"We rejoice in our sufferings, knowing that suffering produces
endurance, and endurance produces character, and character

produces hope, and hope does not put us to shame, because God's love has been poured into our hearts through the Holy Spirit who has been given to us" (Romans 5:3-5).

Lord, I'm entirely dependent. Impaired. Grumpy. Disabled. Controlled by healthcare. Withdrawn to conserve energy. Focused on self. Afraid. It's hard to feel lovely and loved. Loss of hope and control. You can teach me to live "in the moment," an hour at a time, content. Help me be content. My calendar says,

"Deliver me, Lord, from the snare of self-pity, the lie that I am no longer of value"...because I can't make music or be the wife and mother I want to be. When I cannot do things, I can still be useful—praying, praising, being.

"No sin is worse than the sin of self-pity, because it obliterates God and puts self-interest on the throne." [1]

I need Your daily manna of gospel renewal. Protect me in this depression. Turn despair into joy. My Jesus.

♪♪♪

I need thee, O I need thee,
Ev'ry hour I need thee;
O bless me now,
my Savior, I come to thee.

("I NEED THEE EVERY HOUR," REFRAIN: LOWRY, R., 1872)

♪♪♪

≈

"But he was pierced for our transgressions;
he was crushed for our iniquities;
upon him was the chastisement that brought us peace,
and with his wounds we are healed.
All we like sheep have gone astray;

**we have turned—every one—to his own way;
and the LORD has laid on him
the iniquity of us all" (Isaiah 53:5-6).**

♪♪♪

*My hope is built on nothing less
than Jesus' blood and righteousness;
When darkness veils his lovely face,
I rest on his unchanging grace;
His oath, his covenant, his blood
support me in the whelming flood;
On Christ, the solid rock, I stand:
All other ground is sinking sand.*

("MY HOPE IS BUILT ON NOTHING LESS," MOTE, E., 1834)

♪♪♪

BECAUSE HE LIVES

I can't do anything. Everything I love to do, my calling, my gifts— they're all gone. Why Lord? Why me? Bedridden. Wheelchair. No cure. 29 medications a day. Doctors say we can't help you. I can't walk at all today. I long for heaven. Jesus, I want to be with you. I can't live like this. My husband and girls deserve better. I'm ready to go. I'll take care of it right now.

"I am hard-pressed between the two. My desire is to depart and be with Christ, for that is far better" (Philippians 1:23). Here I come, Lord, to meet You through the doorway of death.

Wait...are those angels singing? The song is so loud!

♪♪♪

*Because He lives, I can face tomorrow.
Because He lives, all fear is gone.
Because I know He holds the future*

and life is worth the living,
just because He lives.[2]

♪♪♪

OK, Lord, I believe You. I'll stay on earth, no matter how awful this feels.

∾

GOD'S RESCUE

Lord, I can't do this. I can't take it anymore. I'm in such agony. "If I can honour Thee more by suffering, and if the loss of my earthly all will bring Thee glory, then so let it be. I refuse the comfort, if it comes in the way of Thine honour."[3]

One day I read, "Call for the elders of the church...let them pray" (James 5:14). Nearly eight years after symptoms began, they gathered around my wheelchair and called upon God's mercy. Many had begged God for my healing for years, even in special faith healing services. But this time, I contracted tonsillitis and a high fever three days later!

Dragging home after five days of hospitalization, I checked emails from support group listservs. By then, home internet had been invented!

Exhausted, I deleted most, but a woman's subject of "tonsils" caught my eye. She shared her daughter's healing story of brain surgery on "cerebellar tonsils." The symptoms mirrored mine! Where was her surgery? Oh, Father, You're kidding me! Johns Hopkins, my new home! My internist rushed my MRI scans to that surgeon. Despite my scans being repeatedly read as normal, he said he could help me. I had the same brainstem herniation as this person. God's answer of "Yes" had come after almost eight years.

By God's grace, brain surgery enabled me to function again as a mommy, wife, musician, and teacher. Hallelujah! Praise explosion comes from what happened next as we ponder His amazing grace poured out for many.

~

GOD'S REIGN IN THE WAITING

Our reigning and ruling God knew all. In nearly eight years of exponential suffering, He comforted me as He revealed Himself to be a good, loving, and wise Father who was "working all things together for good for those who are called according to His purposes" (Romans 8:28). As He waited, He created a pathway of sustaining endurance through His Word and singing songs inspired by His Word, filled with His truth.

God's wait magnified His worthiness.

His faithful providence and sovereign hand ordered it all as a gift of love. My diagnosis and surgery required moving to Baltimore, the invention of home internet, connection to Johns Hopkins, support of Maryland church friends and family who cleaned our house, cared for our children, did our laundry, and held me up with Scripturally saturated emotional support.

Most amazingly, since my surgery and resulting media coverage years ago, many have also been healed as they discover this story. TV shows, newspapers, and magazines shared the story. I spent over a year recovering and talking with desperately sick people. Many found their healing answers as a result. If I had been instantly healed as we had fervently prayed for years, perhaps none of these people would have known their enigmatic, complex symptoms also required brain surgery. Even more remarkable, Jesus drew some to Himself by His saving grace.

Soli Deo Gloria.

~

I'll never forget it. As we interviewed to join a church after moving to a new state, one of the elders asked me, "What is your favorite book of the Bible?" I immediately responded, "Job." He was shocked, but many of Job's words resonated with me throughout my suffering. His words of lament became mine. His battle against the enemy's lies became my battle. In what felt like a progressively hopeless journey, finally yearning for death more than life as Job did, I desperately needed to understand what is true about God and myself as His child, a believer in Christ.

Just as with Job, the Lord never answered me with details of "why," but He answered with Biblical truth about Himself. He replied with comfort and compassion, mingled with gospel-centered realities of what it means to belong to Him, unified with Christ. He responded by reminding me of Scriptures in lonely and pain-filled hospital beds, filling my heart with Scriptural songs. Over and over, He brought a rested peace and surrender to His sovereign and loving care, regardless of outcomes.

The Lord helped me find hope in my suffering through the gospel of Jesus Christ. Like Job in his wrestling and worsening hopelessness, I battled for hope by interrupting my suffering experience with outbursts of truth and praise to our God, but all by His Spirit's work. My pain-full questions came first, and the book of Job offered the Lord's answers to me...and to all of us who suffer in our earthly lives.

∼

In the providential timing and compassionate care of God, I wrote most of this book before a new chapter in my own life story. As the first draft finished, my physical suffering began escalating again, a reprise of what happened in the 90s. My story continues to hold a song of *praise interruptions*, in sung prayers to our heavenly Father, into my suffering.

This book ended up ministering to my suffering heart in the editing process. Our Lord of love used the Scriptures I'll share with you to speak grace to my soul, into fresh tears and fears accompanying my body's challenges.

SOME HELPFUL INSTRUCTIONS

I pray that this book will help answer your many questions and that your journey of suffering will be a uniquely special time of God's abundant grace. Grab a journal and pen if you're reading a digital version of this book.

As you come to the Scriptures, you'll be invited to feast on milk, bread, and a meal. Enjoy the milk verses if you only have time or energy for a quick milkshake, looking up 1-2 Scriptures! If you have more time, add a bite of warm bread. If you have even more time and ability, feast on a full meal.

You will sometimes notice repeated Scriptures woven throughout the study. This is intentional. As we read something repetitively, perhaps on a different day with a different experience of suffering on that day, the Lord might use it differently for our hearts. Repetition also promotes memorization. He tells us to hide His Word in our hearts (Psalm 119:11), and the Holy Spirit will bring Scripture to your mind and heart, perhaps tucked away through repetition. If a particular Scripture seems to be a truth He is highlighting for you, speak it, write it, pray it, make up a melody to it, or find a composed song with it online! This is His living and active Word to you, dear friend (Hebrews 4:12)!

This study has no time element, so as the Holy Spirit leads you, take your time. My best advice is to be consistent! Don't stop! The Lord will give you strength. Your suffering and pain are your special-hard context to come to Jesus right now, as you sing the gospel to your own heart, as we together "sing the gospel to Job."

"May the God of hope fill you with all joy and peace in believing, so that by the power of the Holy Spirit you may abound in hope" (Romans 15:13).

1

AM I STILL A BELIEVER IF I'M SUFFERING?

*B*eloved in Christ, when we suffer, the enemy continues his wearying lie, "Did God actually say?" (Genesis 3:1). Moments of doubt and fear creep into our thoughts when we're gripped in the lonely pain of suffering. "Doesn't suffering mean that my faith has failed? That I have unconfessed sin causing this? That I'm not strong enough a believer? Oh God, what if I'm *not* a believer? Is that what this trial means?"

In the pain of his prolonged agony, Job's most tremendous pain dwelt here. More than his physical, financial, and relational suffering, he was concerned that God was accusing him and that he was no longer God's. Through his friends' warped views of suffering, the accuser insidiously provoked Job to think it must be his personal and unconfessed sin causing his suffering and that it must be his punishment for his sinful offenses to God. He became afraid that he was not a believer.

The Lord tells us what is true. Right to Satan's face, He called Job "blameless, upright" and a man of "integrity" (1:1, 8; 2:3). Job's inward faith matched his outward words and actions. Although he was not sinless, because we are all born sinners, God proclaimed Job was His believing child. God bragged on him!

No, Job was suffering *because* he was a mature believer. We need to start with a solid foundation of our fixed position as those who are in Christ, as we suffer.

Let's attack lies with Scripture, in the exact way Jesus did: "It is written" (Luke 4:4). Let's sing the gospel to Job and our hearts, finding assured, confident, and expectant hope in Jesus Christ, into our suffering.

～

List some truths you want to remember from the verses below.

> **Lie:** My suffering means I am not right before God and am not saved. "What is man, that he can be pure? Or he who is born of a woman, that he can be righteous?" (Job 15:14)
> **Truth:** No one can be right before God, outside of His gift of grace found in salvation through Jesus Christ. If we are saved, He has made us new creations in Christ (2 Corinthians 5:17).

Milk: Romans 3:23; Romans 5:8; Romans 10:9

Bread: Ephesians 2:1-2; Romans 6:23; Romans 5:1

Meal: 1 Corinthians 15:3-4; 1 John 5:11-12; Romans 8:1

> **Lie:** Believers aren't supposed to go through suffering, only wicked nonbelievers. "The wicked man writhes in pain all his

days, through all the years that are laid up for the ruthless" (Job 15:20).
Truth: Believers must and always do go through suffering in this fallen world. We follow in the footsteps of Jesus, who suffered and died for us.

Milk: 1 Peter 4:12-13; Romans 8:16-17

Bread: Acts 14:22; 2 Corinthians 1:5

Meal: 2 Timothy 3:12; 1 Peter 2:21

Lie: My suffering will never end. It's hopeless. "Where then is my hope? Who will see my hope?" (Job 17:15)
Truth: Suffering will completely disappear in the new heaven and earth—when all things are restored, Satan is permanently destroyed, and all sin is eradicated. We're waiting for this inheritance because God has given us persevering faith through His indwelling Spirit!

Milk: 1 Peter 5:10; Revelation 21:1-7

Bread: Romans 8:10-11, 14-16

Meal: 1 Corinthians 1:8; Ephesians 1:3-11

My prayer to You, my Savior, my Redeemer, my glorious Lord

In my suffering, You say this is true:

So, in my suffering, I praise You because:

In my suffering, please help me with:

Into my suffering, I'll sing these songs from my playlist today:

♪♪♪

I hear the Savior say,
"Your strength indeed is small,
child of weakness, watch and pray,
find in me your all in all."

Jesus paid it all,
all to him I owe;
sin had left a crimson stain,
he washed it white as snow.

Lord, now indeed I find
your power, and yours alone,
can change the leper's spots,
and melt the heart of stone.

For nothing good have I
whereby your grace to claim —
I'll wash my garments white
in the blood of Calv'ry's lamb.

And when, before the throne,
I stand in him complete,
"Jesus died my soul to save,"
my lips shall still repeat.

("Jesus Paid It All," Hall, E. M., 1865)

♪♪♪

2

HOW CAN A GOOD AND LOVING
GOD LET THIS HAPPEN TO ME?

*I*ncluding Job and myself, I don't know one person who's experienced deep suffering and has not asked this question in the throes of pain and absolute despair. Perhaps the enemy digs even further...*is* God good and loving? How could He be, if I'm a believer in Christ and yet suffering? Let's settle into some of God's answers as He reveals His unchanging attributes in Scripture.

"God is love" (1 John 4:8), and in Christ, His always-steadfast, enduring, *hesed*, covenant love was shown to us. "But God shows his love for us in that while we were still sinners, Christ died for us" (Romans 5:8). No suffering of any kind, nothing at all, "will be able to separate us from the love of God in Christ Jesus our Lord" (Romans 8:39). On this side of the cross, we can rest assured that God loves us; our suffering does not negate this truth.

God tells us that He is always good. Jesus Himself tells us that God alone is good (Mark 10:18). The Psalmists exhort us to thank God for His unchanging goodness (e.g., Psalms 106, 107, 118. 136), and Psalm 119:68 tells us that God *is* good, and He *does* good. Remember that when He created all things in Genesis, He called them "good?" The

Hebrew for "good" tells us they were valuable, useful, and pleasurable. But then sin entered our good world. So our fallen world of sin needed *good* news. In Christ, God gave us His goodness. This means that when He says, "For those who love God *all* things work together for *good* for those who are called according to his purpose" (Romans 8:28), God's goodness is at work in our lives as believers, His beloved in Christ. In my deepest pain, this is my deepest comfort.

Is God good and loving? He is. But for the worst days of raging storms, let's anchor our hearts with more truth rooted in the gospel, just as Job's words point us to God's goodness and love for us, in Jesus Christ.

～

List some truths you want to remember from the verses below.

> **Lie:** God is angry with me because I'm not good enough. "God will not turn back his anger" (Job 9:13).
> **Truth:** God's anger over my sin was removed from me, placed on Jesus instead of me, because no one (including me) is good enough to enter God's presence. "But now the righteousness of God has been manifested apart from the law" (Romans 3:23). Jesus took all the deserved punishment for my sin, and His perfect righteousness has now been credited to me. Those who have trusted in Jesus Christ for salvation don't need to fear God is angry with us when we suffer.

Milk: Romans 8:1-2; Romans 5:9

Bread: Romans 3:25-26; 1 John 4:18

Meal: 1 Thessalonians 5:9; Ephesians 2:1-10

Lie: God must have abandoned me because I can't feel Him. "Behold, he passes by me, and I see him not; he moves on, but I do not perceive him" (Job 9:11).
Truth: God is always within those who have put their trust in Christ for salvation, by His indwelling Holy Spirit, "who has also put his seal on us and given us his Spirit in our hearts as a guarantee" (2 Corinthians 1:22).

Milk: Ephesians 1:13-14

Bread: 1 John 4:4; Romans 8:26-27

Meal: Psalm 139

Lie: God is accusing me, and I'm afraid of His punishment... there's no one to argue my case (Job 9:33-35).
Truth: Jesus is my mediator, so I have peace with God because I'm in Christ. "For there is one God, and there is one mediator between God and men, the man Christ Jesus" (1 Timothy 2:5).

Milk: 1 John 4:13-18

Bread: Hebrews 12:21-24, 28

Meal: John 15:13-15

Lie: God will make this go away if I have enough faith, confess my sin, or pray the right way (Job 11:13-19; 22:21-30).
Truth: I can trust and hope in God's goodness and love whether my earthly suffering ends or not because it will end one day for a believer in Christ...in the new heaven and earth!

Milk: John 14:3; Romans 5:3-5

Bread: 1 Peter 1:3-7

Meal: 2 Corinthians 4:16-18

My prayer to You, Father, Son, and Holy Spirit

In my suffering, You say this is true:

So, in my suffering, I praise You because:

In my suffering, please help me with:

Into my suffering, I'll sing these songs from my playlist today:

♪♪♪

My hope is built on nothing less
than Jesus' blood and righteousness;
I dare not trust the sweetest frame,
but wholly lean on Jesus' name.

On Christ, the solid rock, I stand;
all other ground is sinking sand;
all other ground is sinking sand.

When darkness veils his lovely face,
I rest on his unchanging grace;
in every high and stormy gale
my anchor holds within the veil.

His oath, his covenant, his blood
support me in the whelming flood;
when all around my soul gives way,
he then is all my hope and stay.

When he shall come with trumpet sound,
O may I then in him be found;
dressed in his righteousness alone,
faultless to stand before the throne.

("MY HOPE IS BUILT ON NOTHING LESS," MOTE, E., 1834)

♪♪♪

3

WHAT ABOUT SATAN AND EVIL?

*A*m I being attacked by Satan when I suffer? The evil of suffering becomes horrifically frightening when we wonder if God is powerful over evil and Satan. Let's find great comfort in God's Word together.

What a loving Father to open a tiny window into His throne room.

"And the Lord said to Satan, 'Behold, all that [Job] has is in your hand. Only against him do not stretch out your hand.' So Satan went out from the presence of the Lord" (Job 1:12).

"And the Lord said to Satan, 'Behold, [Job] is in your hand; only spare his life'" (Job 2:6).

Before Satan could inflict Job, he had to ask God Almighty for permission. Satan had to *obey* God because God set tight boundaries. This means Satan is *not* God's equal; he's simply one of God's created beings who fell. Let's battle Satan's lies together! The enemy wants us to think he's as powerful as God and that evil wins as I suffer, but what is true?

~

List some truths you want to remember from the verses below.

Lie: Satan is all-powerful and controls things that happen.
Truth: God is powerful over Satan, who is simply a rebellious created angel. Satan only attacks a believer with God's tight permission. Satan is like a little whiny pet dog on a leash (Leviathan) in our God's mighty hand! Job's response to learning this was settled and repentant worship of our great God.

Milk: Job 41:5 & 11

Bread: Luke 4:33-36; Luke 8:27-33

Meal: Psalm 103:19; Isaiah 46:9-11; Ephesians 1:14-21

Lie: So, God has total power over Satan. But there's no possible good purpose to the suffering God's allowing in my life.
Truth: God uses Satan's evil purposes for good reasons in the life of a Christian. The most significant example of this is the evil inflicted upon Jesus as He died on the cross, enduring abandonment from the Father, for us, the worst suffering known to anyone (Mark 15:34). And what was its good and higher purpose? "For God so loved the world, that he gave his only Son, that whoever believes in him should not perish but have eternal life" (John 3:16).

Milk: Genesis 50:20-21; 1 Peter 1:5-7; 2 Corinthians 4:16-17

Bread: Romans 8:28

. . .

Meal: 2 Corinthians 12:7

Lie: There's nothing I can do when Satan is trying to make me doubt God's goodness and love.
Truth: I can praise God for who He is, as He's shown in His Word, and for what He's done for me in the gospel of Jesus Christ. I'm battling the lies right now as I read His Word! Knowing His Word deeply will help me resist Satan's lies. This time of suffering is my particular time to dig into Scripture.

Milk: 1 Peter 5:6-9

Bread: Ephesians 6:10-13

Meal: Ephesians 6:14-18

Lie: Satan is going to win this battle.
Truth: Jesus has already won! In the very end, the Lord will permanently remove Satan and evil, forever.

Milk: Referring to His death on the cross, Jesus says this in John 12:31:

According to Revelation 12:7-12, this happened at the cross, when salvation came to this world:

Colossians 2:15 (This is what Jesus did on the cross, referring back to Ephesians 6:12):

. . .

Bread: Hebrews 2:14-15

Meal: Revelation 20:10; Matthew 25:31-34, 41; Romans 16:20

My prayer to You, all-powerful God, my loving and good Father

In my suffering, You say this is true:

So, in my suffering, I praise You because:

In my suffering, please help me with:

Into my suffering, I'll sing these songs from my playlist today:

♪♪♪

A mighty fortress is our God,
a bulwark never failing;
our helper he amid the flood of mortal ills prevailing.
For still our ancient foe doth seek to work us woe;
his craft and pow'r are great;
and armed with cruel hate,
on earth is not his equal.

Did we in our own strength confide,
our striving would be losing;
were not the right man on our side, the man of God's own choosing.
Dost ask who that may be?
Christ Jesus, it is he,
Lord Sabaoth his name,
from age to age the same,
and he must win the battle.

And though this world, with devils filled,
should threaten to undo us,
we will not fear, for God hath willed his truth to triumph through us.
The prince of darkness grim, we tremble not for him;
his rage we can endure,
for lo! his doom is sure;
one little word shall fell him.

That Word above all earthly pow'rs,
no thanks to them, abideth;
the Spirit and the gifts are ours through him who with us sideth.
Let goods and kindred go, this mortal life also;
the body they may kill:
God's truth abideth still;
his kingdom is forever.

("A MIGHTY FORTRESS IS OUR GOD," LUTHER, M., 1529; TRANS. HEDGE, F. H., 1852)

♪♪♪

4

WHAT ABOUT PRAYER?

*J*ob's friends filled him with our accuser's lies about prayer. They told him he wasn't praying right because God wasn't coming through with a "yes" answer (22:27-28). They warned him that he must have unconfessed sin blocking the way to healing and prosperity (22:22-26). They instructed him that if we believe, decide, agree with God, or declare strongly enough, God will make it happen for us (22:21). As time dragged on, these lies wore him into despair...maybe God wasn't hearing him because God was not fixing things (30:16-20).

Sound familiar? The lies of the accuser haven't changed at all. As Job's story concludes, God warns that his friends "have not spoken of me what is right, as my servant Job has" (42:7-8). We must listen to God's teaching about prayer rather than the lies of the accuser...or perhaps well-meaning friends who hate to see us suffer and make false claims about prayer.

Our heavenly Father tells us to ask for what we need (Matthew 7:7-11), to pray without ceasing (1 Thessalonians 5:17), to cast all our anxieties on Him because He cares for us (1 Peter 5:7), to pray for others, including our enemies (Luke 6:28), and that His ears are open to the prayers of the righteous (1 Peter 3:12). For those clothed in the righteousness of Jesus Christ as Savior, that is you and me. In fact, Jesus Himself is interceding for us through His Spirit when we don't even know how to pray or what to pray for (Romans 8:26-27, 34). God tells us to pray when we're suffering and to ask for prayer as we suffer (James 5:13-18).

But it is not the quality of our prayers or faith that give us "yes" answers. Prayer is not an "if-then" formula to get God to do what we want Him to do. Let's remember Whom we are praying to and why we pray to Him. Our prayers of pain or lament are prayers of deep intimacy and trust in our Father of love who is also the sovereign, thrice holy, and trustworthy God of power who can do anything according to His nature and purpose. And He does, in His perfect time and manner. So, let's look at some Scriptures to understand better the role of prayer as we talk with God in our suffering.

～

List some truths you want to remember from the verses below.

Lie: God can't fix my suffering.
Truth: God is the sovereign, powerful, mighty, wise, good, loving, strong, holy, perfect I AM. He can do anything.

Milk: Job 38

Bread: Job 39

Meal: Job 40-41

Lie: God doesn't hear me. He's forgotten me, abandoned me.
Truth: God is always with a true believer in Christ, by His indwelling Spirit.

Milk: Matthew 28:20

Bread: Deuteronomy 31:6; 1 Corinthians 3:16

Meal: Romans 8:9-11, 14-17, 35-39

Lie: I know what's best for me and my life.
Truth: Only God knows what's best for me and my life, as His beloved child, in Christ. His purpose for my life is to conform me to the image of Christ (Romans 8:29), glorifying Him (John 15:8). So I join Jesus, my Savior, in praying, "Thy will be done."

Milk: 1 Peter 4:12-13; Mark 14:35-36

Bread: Romans 11:33-36

Meal: Romans 8:29-30; 2 Corinthians 3:18 & 4:16-18

Lie: God isn't answering, "yes," so there's something wrong with my faith or my prayers.
Truth: God sometimes answers with "wait, not yet" or "no, my beloved child." We often don't pray according to His will for this time in our lives.

Milk: Psalm 115:3; Isaiah 40:28-31

Bread: 1 Peter 4:19; 1 John 5:14-15; James 4:2-3

Meal: Proverbs 3:5; Romans 5:1-5; 1 Peter 5:6-7

My prayer to You, God Almighty, who is my Abba Father

In my suffering, You say this is true:

So, in my suffering, I praise You because:

In my suffering, please help me with:

Into my suffering, I'll sing these songs from my playlist today:

♪♪♪

Have thine own way, Lord! Have thine own way!
Thou art the potter; I am the clay.
Mold me and make me after thy will,
while I am waiting, yielded and still.

Have thine own way, Lord! Have thine own way!
Search me and try me, Master, today!
Whiter than snow, Lord, wash me just now,
as in thy presence humbly I bow.

Have thine own way, Lord! Have thine own way!
Wounded and weary, help me, I pray!
Power, all power, surely is thine!
Touch me and heal me, Savior divine!

Have thine own way, Lord! Have thine own way!
Hold o'er my being absolute sway!
Fill with thy Spirit till all shall see
Christ only, always, living in me!

("HAVE THINE OWN WAY, LORD," POLLARD, A. A., 1906)

♪♪♪

5

WHY IS THERE SUFFERING IN A BELIEVER'S LIFE?

$\mathcal{L}$ike Job, we cry out to God, "Why?" We wrestle with God's possible purpose of suffering in our lives. Job's cries of "why" reflected his fears that God was judging him. "Why do you hide your face and count me as your enemy?" (13:24). "I will say to God, Do not condemn me; let me know why you contend against me" (10:2). Job repeatedly cried words of "Why am I even alive?" in his agony and despair (3:11-12, 20, 23, 26; 9:29; 10:18).

As Job's friends fed his hopelessness, Job never sinned in his "why" questions. Neither do we. As Jesus was genuinely forsaken by our Father on the cross, bearing the required punishment for our sin, our sinless Savior lamented, "My God, my God, why have you forsaken me?" (Matthew 27:46). Even if our "why" questions were sin, on this side of the cross, believers in Jesus Christ can rest assured that we are not forsaken because "there is therefore now no condemnation for those who are in Christ Jesus" (Romans 8:1).

By His great grace, He made us new creations in Christ (2 Corinthians 5:17) and "has delivered us from the domain of darkness and transferred us to the kingdom of his beloved Son, in whom we have redemption, the forgiveness of sins" (Colossians 1:13-14).

We once were enemies of God, but "God shows his love for us in that while we were still sinners, Christ died for us" (Romans 5:8), and "since we have been justified by faith, we have peace *with* God through our Lord Jesus Christ" (Romans 5:1, emphasis added). We are no longer His enemies.

But we often seek Him as Job did, in agony and despair, with "why" questions. Praise God, He's given us so many possible answers in Scripture. He knows our needs, so He graciously gives us answers. Let's discover some of our loving Father's possible reasons why this could be happening.

∼

List some truths you want to remember from the verses below.

> **Lie:** There are no good purposes for our earthly suffering
> **Truth:** Suffering helps us become more reliant or dependent on God, like Jesus.

Milk: Psalm 10:17; Hebrews 5:7-9

Bread: Matthew 10:38-39; 16:24

Meal: Philippians 3:10; 2 Corinthians 1:8-9

> **Lie:** There are no good purposes for our earthly suffering.

Truth: God has fruit-bearing, kingdom purposes for all that happens in a believer's life, like Jesus.

Milk: Isaiah 46:10: Philippians 1:6

Bread: John 12:24-28; Hebrews 2:10

Meal: John 15:8; Hebrews 12:5-6, 10-11

Lie: My suffering must mean I'm a weak and faithless Christian.
Truth: Through His continual grace and power by His indwelling Spirit, suffering produces strong faith and a deepened relationship with Him, in those who are in Jesus Christ and becoming conformed to His image.

Milk: 2 Corinthians 4:7-10

Bread: 1 Peter 5:8; James 1:2-4

Meal: 2 Corinthians 12:8-10; James 1:12

Lie: My suffering is too ugly and painful to have a good purpose.
Truth: Like a surgeon or sculptor bringing healing and beauty, God is transforming, shaping, changing, and refining us into His beautiful and holy image, more like Jesus.

Milk: Proverbs 27:21; Isaiah 48:10; Ephesians 4:13

Bread: 2 Corinthians 3:18; Titus 2:12-14

Meal: Isaiah 32:17; Philippians 4:11-13

My prayer to You, beautiful and perfect Father

In my suffering, You say this is true:

So, in my suffering, I praise You because:

In my suffering, please help me with:

Into my suffering, I'll sing these songs from my playlist today:

♪♪♪

How firm a foundation, you saints of the Lord,
is laid for your faith in his excellent Word!
What more can he say than to you he has said,
to you who for refuge to Jesus have fled?

"Fear not, I am with you, O be not dismayed;
for I am your God, and will still give you aid;
I'll strengthen you, help you, and cause you to stand,
upheld by my righteous, omnipotent hand.

When through the deep waters I call you to go,
the rivers of sorrow shall not overflow;
for I will be with you, your troubles to bless,
and sanctify to you your deepest distress.

When through fiery trials your pathway shall lie,
my grace, all-sufficient, shall be your supply;
the flame shall not hurt you; I only design
your dross to consume and your gold to refine.

E'en down to old age all my people shall prove
my sovereign, eternal, unchangeable love;
and when hoary hairs shall their temples adorn,
like lambs they shall still in my bosom be borne.

"The soul that on Jesus has leaned for repose,
I will not, I will not desert to his foes;
that soul, though all hell should endeavor to shake,
I'll never, no never, no never forsake."

("HOW FIRM A FOUNDATION," K., 1787)

♪♪♪

6

DOESN'T GOD WANT TO HEAL HIS CHILDREN?

As one who has begged God for healing over many years of progressively worsening illness in my own life, Job feels like a fellow chronic illness friend to me. He dealt with chronic pain and visible skin issues that were itchy, infected, and gross. He had no appetite and lost weight, with fevers and breathing challenges. Insomnia and depression affected his brain with cascading neurochemical reactions. Check out chapters 2, 7, 16, 19, 29 30 for gruesome details.

In Job's despair, he didn't ask God to heal him of symptoms, but he freely complained, "I loathe my life" (10:1). In His spiritual agony of responding to the lies and trying to figure out what sin he'd done to cause this, he soon after begged God for comfort and a break from it all. It is God's healing mercy when we experience moments of relief, however short they feel.

We know God *can* heal because our powerful and sovereign God can do anything. Sometimes, He asks, "Do you believe that I am *able* to do this?" (Matthew 9:28, emphasis added). This is faith in His ability. Of course, all of us have experienced the healing of Jehovah Rapha (Exodus

15:26). God has healed the tiniest paper cut, a headache, the flu, or provided a needed surgery.

But He also shows us we must humbly ask for His perfect way and will, submitting to His authority and purpose. I've wrestled with this. Am I putting my faith in God's healing my body? Or am I trusting in God Himself? He has gently taught me that we must come to our loving Father as the leper came to Jesus and said, "*If* you will..." (Mark 1:40) and as Jesus Himself modeled for us, "Father, *if* you are willing, remove this cup from me. Nevertheless, not my will, but *yours* be done" (Luke 22:42). And we rest there. "You have granted me life and steadfast love, and your care has preserved my spirit" (Job 10:12).

Jesus healed as mercy (Matthew 20:30), with pity (Matthew 20:34), to show people that He was indeed God who has authority over all (Mark 2:1-10; Luke 4:31-37). Although Jesus compassionately healed many, multitudes clamored for miracle healings...and yet He only healed some. Instead of healing Lazarus, Jesus let him die. Then He created Lazarus anew when He called him out of the tomb (John 11); our Lord had a far greater purpose than instant healing. Sometimes, He was supposed to move on to other towns to preach the gospel instead (Mark 1:35-39). Sometimes He healed people without their even asking for it (Luke 13:10-13). Remember that He walked to a pool crowded with chronically ill people and chose to heal only one of them (John 5:1-17)? So, what do we do with this reality? What do we do with these clearly different varieties of Jesus' actions, remembering that "Jesus is the same, yesterday, today, and forever" (Hebrews 13:8)?

We trust Him for His sufficient grace.

As we continually pray for Him to fix our broken bodies and keep trying various treatments, sometimes God does say "no" or "wait" because it's not His perfect will to heal our bodies right now. If He didn't answer this way, no one would ever die! In our earthly years of non-body-healing and the discouragement it can bring, let's rest in our loving Father's answer: "My grace is sufficient for you, for my power is *made perfect* in weakness" (2 Corinthians 12:9, emphasis added).

∽

Made perfect. God is perfecting or completing us, just as He made Jesus "perfect through suffering" (Hebrews 2:10). For a believer, the stripes afflicted on Jesus, our beloved Savior, have already permanently healed us. 1 Peter explains what this actually means...it has to do with our sin. Our sinful hearts were healed the moment the Lord saved us from His just punishment, justified us, made us right with Him, and gave us new hearts. God's works of salvation were brought to completion through Jesus' suffering...for you and me.

So, we are healed or "made whole," now and forever...even if our bodies aren't. Although sickness, an effect of sin in this fallen world, feels like miserable suffering for us, He has healed our souls now and forever. Because God often brings His beloved children home through sickness and resulting death, His healing of our bodies might happen when "the righteous man is taken away from calamity; he enters into peace" (Isaiah 57:1-2). When God restores all things in the new heaven and earth, "He will wipe away every tear from their eyes, and death shall be no more, neither shall there be...pain anymore, for the former things have passed away" (Revelation 21:4). How we long for that day, don't we? Our bodies will be perfectly restored! It's His promise! By His stripes, we *are* healed!

As we both pray for physical healing and keep seeking His answers for relief and comfort, let's cling to the spiritual healing God's already given us through the person and work of Jesus Christ. Let's rest in and obediently submit to His perfect healing work and grace-filled timing in our lives, knowing that our suffering is bringing about His healing. Let's cast all our anxieties on Him because He cares for us, beloved in Christ (1 Peter 5:7).

∽

List some truths you want to remember from the verses below.

Lie: God *promises* physical healing for believers throughout our earthly life, in the timing and ways we desire.
Truth: God promises complete *spiritual* healing from our sin. He also gives us physical healing as He desires, wills, and chooses.

Milk: Isaiah 53:4-8; 1 Peter 2:21-25

Bread: Romans 8:22-25; 2 Corinthians 5:1-5

Meal: Philippians 4:12-13; James 5:14-15

My prayer to You, my healing Father

In my suffering, You say this is true:

So, in my suffering, I praise You because:

In my suffering, please help me with:

Into my suffering, I'll sing these songs from my playlist today:

♪♪♪

My faith has found a resting place,
from guilt my soul is freed;
I trust the ever-living One,
his wounds for me shall plead.

I need no other argument,
I need no other plea,
it is enough that Jesus died,
and that he died for me.

Enough for me that Jesus saves,
this ends my fear and doubt;
a sinful soul I come to him,
he'll never cast me out.

My heart is leaning on the Word,
the written Word of God:
salvation by my Savior's name,
salvation thro' his blood.

My great Physician heals the sick,
the lost he came to save;
for me his precious blood he shed,
for me his life he gave.

("MY FAITH HAS FOUND A RESTING PLACE," EDMUNDS, L. H., 1891)

♪♪♪

7

I WANT TO UNDERSTAND MY SUFFERING

*L*et's get past the harmful and destructive lies of Job's friends, mingled with truth bursts, wearing Job down to hopelessness. Their sinful arrogance and pride made them think they could understand God's reasons behind another person's suffering! Sometimes well-meaning, but judgmental people (like Job's friends) inform us that we need more faith or need to pray better. They told Job he could coerce God to remove suffering and get blessings if he repented correctly and believed. Remember that God rebukes all of this false teaching about who God is and who we are, in Job 42:7-9.

Just like Job, we agonize over making sense of our suffering, don't we? As we've seen, His Word gives us many possible answers for its meaning. But ultimately, we need to fight the lies as Job did, coming to the foundational character of God, now shown to us in the person and work of Jesus Christ. The answer is God Himself.

As those who are in union with Jesus Christ, God helps us deal with earthly suffering through who He *is*. We can't fully understand because we're mere humans, but we can trust Him. He's our Abba Father now. We may never understand while on earth, but we have hope and complete security in our righteousness that is in Christ. "I hold fast my righteousness and will not let it go" (Job 27:6). Just as Job dug into this truth, so must we.

~

Let's remember the gospel! Jesus bore all of God's just, totally fair wrath for our inborn sin, and He has given us His righteousness instead (2 Corinthians 5:21). Yes, we still sin, but He's even taking away our sinful desires because He's made us new creations in Christ (2 Corinthians 5:17), and He's now using the faith He's given to us to conform us more and more into the image of Christ (Romans 8:29). He will complete and accomplish His work (Philippians 1:6). So, our understanding gradually comes as we humbly turn our eyes to Jesus, who suffered and died in our place. We are "in Christ" (1 Corinthians 15:22), literally moved from this earth's darkness and transferred into the kingdom of Jesus Christ (Colossians 1:13). It's mysterious and wonderful, even as we walk through suffering in our earthly phase of life.

It means that any understanding of our suffering is bathed in His love for those *in Christ*. Our last hymn sang, "It is enough that Jesus died and that He died for me." I had to come to grips with this. In my desperate desire to understand, my aching heart finally realized, like Job, that we can't fully know God's reasons...because we aren't God. I had to recognize that God's blessings on earth are gifts of His grace, not rewards for my faith or good behavior.

So...is it enough that Jesus died for me? Is He enough, even if my suffering continues on earth? Can I say with Job, "Though he slay me, I will hope in him" (13:15)? Can I rest in my close relationship with God, like Job, rather than obsessing over the blessings I want Him to give me? Is God enough? God permitted Satan to attack Job because Satan wanted to prove God was *not enough* for Job! Satan snickered, "Remove God's obvious blessings and see what happens!"

Beloved, could this be our test as well?

. . .

"If God is for us, who can be against us? Who shall bring any charge against God's elect? It is God who justifies. Who is to condemn? Christ Jesus is the one who died—more than that, who was raised—who is at the right hand of God, who indeed is interceding for us" (Rom. 8:31, 33-34).

Suffering is so hard. How we need Jesus' interceding prayers because Satan continues to tempt us to sin in our pride and unbelief. As the accuser did with Job, he tempts us to try to demand or declare into existence what we want from God or even accuse Him of wrongdoing in our lives. And, as with Job, these are matters for repentance. "I know that you can do all things, and that no purpose of yours can be thwarted...I have uttered what I did not understand, things too wonderful for me...therefore I despise myself, and repent in dust and ashes" (42:2-3, 5).

So, let's battle sin with His indwelling Spirit's help, by continuing to return to the cross of Jesus and His abundant grace to us, worshiping and adoring God for who He is, and trusting His purposes because we love Him, and He loves us. Beloved, let's remember daily...He showed us on the cross.

∼

List some truths you want to remember from the verses below.

Lie: My suffering is unfair (Job 19:6-10).
Truth: God is never unfair but is always fair, trustworthy, and just.

Milk: Deuteronomy 32:4; Isaiah 30:18

Bread: Romans 3:23-26

. . .

Meal: Job 36:22-26; Job 37:23-24

Lie: We're able to understand our suffering completely.
Truth: God's vast wisdom and greatness aren't completely understandable by humans.

Milk: Psalm 145:3; Job 28:28

Bread: Romans 11:33-36

Meal: Job 37:8-14; Deuteronomy 29:29

Lie: My suffering is something I need to concentrate on and control. It's my identity.
Truth: God is in control, and I am in Christ! My identity is *in Christ*! No matter what I suffer on earth, God is also my loving, good, comforting heavenly Father. I can focus on Him, only by His grace!

Milk: Job 42:2-3; Philippians 3:14; Colossians 1:13

Bread: 2 Corinthians 1:3-5; Ephesians 2:13

Meal: Ephesians 3:14-21; Colossians 3:1-4; 1 Peter 5:10

My prayer to You, my wise, sovereign, trustworthy Father

In my suffering, You say this is true:

So, in my suffering, I praise You because:

In my suffering, please help me with:

Into my suffering, I'll sing these songs from my playlist today:

♪♪♪

I am not skilled to understand
what God has willed, what God has planned;
I only know that at his right hand
is One who is my Savior!

I take him at his word indeed:
"Christ died for sinners," this I read;
for in my heart I find a need
of him to be my Savior!

That he should leave his place on high
and come for sinful man to die,
you count it strange? So once did I,
before I knew my Savior!

And oh, that he fulfilled may see
the travail of his soul in me,
and with his work contented be,
as I with my dear Savior!

Yes, living, dying, let me bring
my strength, my solace from this spring;
that he who lives to be my King
once died to be my Savior.

("I AM NOT SKILLED TO UNDERSTAND," GREENWELL, D., 1873)

♪♪♪

8

DOES GOD UNDERSTAND HOW HARD THIS IS FOR ME EMOTIONALLY?

*J*ob cries to God with honesty, in lament. "I will speak in the anguish of my spirit; I will complain in the bitterness of my soul" (7:11). He tells God everything he's feeling. As his friends heaped on lying accusations that worsened his suffering battle, provoking increased shame and multiplied guilt, his frustration and grief became emotions of despair and hopelessness. His feelings took over 24/7. He had no way out. He didn't know what to do, his entire life plan felt destroyed, and he got to the point of asking why he was still alive. He wondered why he was even born (10:18-22). In today's terms, he may have been diagnosed with depression. Not only did he suffer for an expanded length of time, he saw death as rest for the weary even though he didn't have as clear an understanding of everlasting life in Christ as we do.

Do Job's words echo your soul, heart, and emotions today?

"Why is light given to him who is in misery, and life to the bitter in soul, who long for death, but it comes not?" (3:20-21). "My face is red with weeping, and on my eyelids is deep darkness, although...my prayer is pure" (16:16). "Today also my complaint is bitter, my hand is heavy on account of my groaning" (23:1). "And now my soul is poured out within me; days of affliction have taken hold of me...my lyre is turned to mourning, and my pipe to the voice of those who weep" (30:16, 31).

~

God made us emotional beings, housed in a body with a mind that thinks. We are holistically created in the image of God Himself. Beloved in Christ, God understands our emotions. Many faithful children of God (e.g., Moses, Elijah, and David) also experienced emotional suffering. I wonder if we have laments in Job and other places of Scripture (like the Psalms) to show us that God compassionately understands our feelings in suffering by including them in His inspired Word. But He also came to earth to live in a body like ours, incarnated as God the Son, fully experiencing emotions and thoughts as we do, yet in a sinless life. Emotion is not sin; we can freely share how we feel with our loving God.

Hard, ongoing, perhaps lifelong suffering brings relentless waves of emotion, doesn't it? Our Suffering Servant, our Savior, is right there with us in our embodied emotional tears, our longing for relief, and our groans of pain. Let's remember. "Being in agony he prayed more earnestly; and his sweat became like great drops of blood falling down to the ground" (Luke 22:44). So, let's allow our emotions to bring us to Jesus; He also needed to honestly pour out His emotions to our Father every day of His earthly life of suffering. He suffered far more than we ever could...for us.

God understands.

As we continually tell our Lord how we feel throughout the day, hearing Him speaking back to us by His Spirit's illumination of His Word, we realize we're mysteriously connected to Jesus in His suffering. "For as we share abundantly in Christ's sufferings, so through Christ we share abundantly in comfort too" (2 Corinthians 1:5). We discover that our "Father of mercies and God of all comfort...comforts us in all our affliction" (2 Corinthians 1:3-4), just as He comforted our Savior. Let's hear His soft and tender voice as we come to our comforting God.

List some truths you want to remember from the verses below.

Lie: I can never be happy again.
Truth: Even in unending suffering, God helps us emotionally.

Milk: Psalm 34:18; Psalm 86:1-7; Psalm 94:19

Bread: Philippians 4:6-7; Matthew 5:3-5

Meal: Matthew 11:28-29; 2 Thessalonians 2:16-17

Lie: True believers aren't depressed or anxious in times of loss and suffering.
Truth: True believers can be led and carried by God through times of deep despair, sadness, depression, anxiety, and emotional pain.

Milk: Psalm 23

Bread: 2 Corinthians 4:8-11

Meal: Matthew 26:39; 2 Corinthians 12:9

Lie: I need to stuff or hide my emotions as I suffer. They're bad.
Truth: Bringing honest emotions to God, reading His Word to hear His voice, is His loving desire for His beloved children.

Milk: Psalm 62:8; Philippians 4:6-7

Bread: Isaiah 26:3; 1 Peter 5:7

Meal: Psalm 56:8; 2 Corinthians 4:17; Revelation 21:4

My prayer to You, the One who understands my emotions

In my suffering, You say this is true:

So, in my suffering, I praise You because:

In my suffering, please help me with:

Into my suffering, I'll sing these songs from my playlist today:

♪♪♪

Safe in the arms of Jesus,
Safe on his gentle breast,
There by his love o'ershaded,
Sweetly my soul shall rest.
Hark! 'tis the voice of angels,
Borne in a song to me,
Over the fields of glory,
Over the jasper sea.

Safe in the arms of Jesus,
Safe on his gentle breast,
There by his love o'ershaded,
Sweetly my soul shall rest.

Safe in the arms of Jesus,
Safe from corroding care,
Safe from the world's temptations,
Sin cannot harm me there.
Free from the blight of sorrow,
Free from my doubts and fears,
Only a few more trials,
Only a few more tears.

Jesus, my heart's dear Refuge,
Jesus has died for me;
Firm on the Rock of Ages
Ever my trust shall be.
Here let me wait with patience,
Wait till the night is o'er,
Wait till I see the morning
Break on the golden shore.

("SAFE IN THE ARMS OF JESUS, CROSBY, F., 1868)

♪♪♪

9

HOW CAN I STAY FAITHFUL
WHEN I FEEL SO WEAK?

Satan attacked Job because he thought he could cause Job to curse God (1:11; 2:5). So the trials were tests of Job's faith, as spiritual battles. When his friends attacked him for what they assumed was unrepentant sin and weak faith, Job fought to defend his spiritual self. One of his fiercest defenses points forward into our current historical time, far beyond Job's lifetime.

"For I know that my Redeemer lives, and at the last he will stand upon the earth" (19:25).

Job fought by looking forward to His Redeemer, who is also *our* Redeemer, Jesus Christ! He has come, He is alive, and He will come again! When Jesus Christ returns to judge, we who are His will have fought "the good fight of the faith" (1 Timothy 6:12) in this very suffering that strengthens our faith. Like Job, we must look forward to the glorious end of history and time as we know it.

∾

Yet, our sufferings are spiritual battles for us too. Some may think that either our easy lives or suffering are indications of our amount of faith or spiritual "strength." That's a lie. Our faith feels so weak, yet He tells us to "be strong in the Lord and in the strength of *his* might" (Ephesians 6:1, emphasis added). Whose might? Who is the source of our faith, from start to finish? "Jesus, the founder and perfecter of our faith" (Hebrews 12:2). This means the Lord will sustain our faith as He takes us to our end: glorification (Romans 8:29-30). Jesus is interceding for us by His Spirit (Romans 8:26-27, 34), the "guarantee of our inheritance" (Ephesians 1:14).

So, in Satan's attacks and lies, how can we stay faithful when we feel weak? First, let's humbly remember and thank Him for our faith. It's all a gift from Him! "By grace you have been saved through faith. And this is not your own doing; it is the gift of God" (Ephesians 2:8). We simply receive as we keep coming to the cross for forgiveness, remembering what He's done, and worshiping our God of grace and love. We look up to Him in the battle. We abide in His love (John 15:9) and ask Him for help to lay aside our sin as He gently convicts us.

We say with Job, "I know that my Redeemer lives!" (19:25). We look at our Savior, who took all our punishment and shame and is now alive and seated on the throne (Hebrews 12:1-2). We remember that Jesus Christ "has gone into heaven and is at the right hand of God, with angels, authorities, and powers having been subjected to him" (1 Peter 3:22)! Our Father of glory "raised him from the dead and seated him at his right hand in the heavenly places, far above all rule and authority and power and dominion" (Ephesians 1:20)!

◞◞

Then, God tells us to "put on the whole armor of God, that you may be able to stand against the schemes of the devil" (Ephesians 6:11). We stand firm (Ephesians 6:13) and resist the lies by submitting ourselves to God (James 4:7). We read and study His Word, the offensive sword of the Spirit (Ephesians 6:17). His Word holds us up, keeps us from tripping, and reminds us of our right standing with God through Christ

(Ephesians 6:14), found in the gospel of Jesus Christ (Ephesians 6:15). No matter what happens, this mighty and robust shield of faith, given to us in Christ, is one we can lift to "extinguish *all* the flaming darts of the evil one" (Ephesians 6:16, emphasis added). We constantly pray, prompted by the Spirit, asking Him to help, "keeping alert with all perseverance" (Ephesians 6:18).

We stay faithful because we have a trustworthy, sovereign, loving God who has given us our faith and will sustain our faith as He sanctifies us completely. "He who calls you is faithful; he will surely do it" (1 Thessalonians 5:24). We will "pass the test" because God is the source of our strength. "And after you have suffered a little while, the God of all grace, who has called you to his eternal glory in Christ, will himself restore, confirm, strengthen, and establish you. To him be the dominion forever and ever. Amen" (1 Peter 5:10-11)!

~

List some truths you want to remember from the verses below.

> **Lie:** I need to create bigger faith somehow to get through this and make it to heaven.
> **Truth:** Jesus has saved believers from God's just punishment and wrath forever. It has nothing to do with the "size" of our faith. Our holy God now sees Jesus' righteousness in us, because He graciously gave us faith in Christ.

Milk: Romans 4:24-5:2

Bread: Romans 5:3-5

Meal: Romans 5:6-11

Lie: I will lose my faith because this suffering is so intense.
Truth: A truly saved believer will not lose faith because God is the source of our faith, no matter how strong the temptation or testing in suffering.

Milk: Ephesians 2:4-7

Bread: Ephesians 2:8-10

Meal: 1 Corinthians 10:13

Lie: I am too weak to endure this.
Truth: God's indwelling Spirit gives us power and strength to endure our suffering.

Milk: Romans 8:26; 2 Corinthians 12:8-9

Bread: John 15:1-11

Meal: Ephesians 3:16-21

My prayer to You, my faithful God of all grace

In my suffering, You say this is true:

So, in my suffering, I praise You because:

In my suffering, please help me with:

Into my suffering, I'll sing these songs from my playlist today:

♪♪♪

My faith looks up to thee,
thou Lamb of Calvary,
Savior divine;
now hear me while I pray,
take all my guilt away,
O let me from this day
be wholly thine.

May thy rich grace impart
strength to my fainting heart,
my zeal inspire;
as thou hast died for me,
O may my love to thee
pure, warm, and changeless be,
a living fire.

While life's dark maze I tread,
and griefs around me spread,
be thou my guide;
bid darkness turn to day,
wipe sorrow's tears away,
nor let me ever stray
from thee aside.

When ends life's transient dream,
when death's cold, sullen stream
shall o'er me roll,
blest Savior, then, in love,
fear and distrust remove;
O bear me safe above,
a ransomed soul.

("MY FAITH LOOKS UP TO THEE," PALMER, R., 1830)

♪♪♪

10

HOW CAN I MAKE IT THROUGH
THIS WITH HOPE?

*H*ow can we maintain hope when our prayers seem to go unanswered for months and years? For me, hope in God's "yes" answer of healing also drove me to obsessive and continual searches for the right treatments and doctors, the proper prayers to pray...the "works" to do that would fix things. It often felt hopeless when years of "no" or "wait" answers happened. At times, Job's words were mine, "What is my strength, that I should wait? And what is my end, that I should be patient? Have I any help in me, when resource is driven from me?" (6:11, 13). As years wore on, hope didn't come from self-care, self-help, or mustering up hope that things would be fixed. In the hard waiting, I finally needed to hope in God Himself, trusting His choice to answer the many thousands of prayers, according to His will.

Job never stopped hoping in the Lord Himself, regardless of the earthly outcome. His honest and angsty prayers show us his more profound hope, even in his hopeless feelings. "You have granted me life and stead-fast love, and your care has preserved my spirit" (10:12). Like with Job, the Lord gives us hope by helping us remember what we know to be true about Him, as we walk in the daily suffering.

But also like Job, we cling to hope in a guaranteed eternal future in God's presence. As Job battled the lies, he burst out with a prophetic foretaste of our own hope in Christ, offering, "And after my skin has been thus destroyed, yet in my flesh I shall see God, whom I shall see for myself, and my eyes shall behold and not another. My heart faints within me!" (19:25-27).

Now that Jesus has risen victorious over sin and death, we hope with even more understanding. Our mighty King has fulfilled His promise to save His people (Zephaniah 3:17), and we are assured of His perfect kingdom's total completion one day. We have complete hope in His kingdom plan! It's His gospel plan! When God created the universe, it was "very good" (Genesis 1:31). But, since the Genesis 3 fall, sin and its effects have ruined everything. We suffer, we sin, we hurt, we die. Romans 8 tells us we're groaning, aching, longing for a world without sin. We're longing to be with Him, but in a sinless world. It's coming! God had a kingdom plan from the beginning!

～

In His beautiful plan, God incarnated as a human who went through the worst of suffering and death, in our place, yet without any sin. And now, Jesus Christ is alive and within us, as sinners saved by His gift of grace. He is our very-much-alive, reigning, and living hope, in Whom we have been born again (1 Peter 1:3). One day, our King will return, will judge and remove all sin, and we will live resurrected with Him forever. Because there will be no more sin or evil, our sorrows will end, our bodies will be perfectly restored, and we will experience wholeness and *shalom* peace in the presence of our Lord. We are waiting...with hope.

A deep and peaceful hope finally comes through daily remembering the gospel. Resting in our eternal hope becomes a sure hope that we're walking through suffering *with* and *in* Christ. It's a hope in Jesus Himself. It's a hope that never changes, regardless of our earthly circumstances changing. Because sometimes...they don't, even though we desire easier and more comfortable circumstances. But we have hope today because God has given us another day in His continual care.

~

In His perfect plan for our lives, He woke us up today for a gospel-centered, kingdom reason! Today is never a given or an assumption. Yet, He tells us that "His mercies never come to an end; they are new every morning" (Lamentations 3:22-23). We don't know what's next, around the corner in the journey He's planned for us. So, we need to find hope in something other than a "yes" answer, even as we pray for it. It's a hope in *Who*, in His unchanging character and His actual Biblical promises for those in His kingdom, rather than a hope in our desires coming true.

What are some of His promises to those in Christ, as we suffer? We have so much earthly hope, even as we suffer on earth and look with assured hope to our eternal home! Here are just a handful:

"I will never leave you, nor forsake you" (Hebrews 13:5).

"I am with you always, to the end of the age" (Matthew 28:20).

"I am the resurrection and the life. Whoever believes in me, though he die, yet shall he live" (John 11:25).

I have a new life (1 John 5:12), and I'm alive...*with* Christ (Romans 6:4-5, 10; Colossians 2:13).

Jesus, by His Spirit, is living within me and is interceding for me (John 15:4; 2 Corinthians 1:19-22; Galatians 2:20; Hebrews 7:25).

Nothing I suffer through can separate me from God's love (Romans 8:35-39).

The Lord is bringing forth fruit in my life (John 15:1-5; Galatians 5:22).

"For God has not destined us for wrath, but to obtain salvation through our Lord Jesus Christ, who died for us so that whether we are awake or asleep we might live *with* him" (1 Thessalonians 5:9-10, emphasis added).

~

List some truths you want to remember from the verses below.

Lie: God promises a peaceful, perfect, comfortable, easy life on earth.
Truth: God promises a peaceful, *shalom*, perfect-in-every-way life in His restored new heaven and earth. He also promises His peace and presence, in the midst of our earthly suffering.

Milk: Romans 8:16-18, 23-25

Bread: Revelation 22:1-5

Meal: Ephesians 1:3-14; Philippians 4:4-9

Lie: If we declare or decide something in prayer, it will happen on earth. So this is our hope.
Truth: Prayer is not a formula to get God to do something we want, but we humbly ask our Father for something we want, as we rest in His perfect will and plan. Our hope is in God, not in our works of prayer.

Milk: John 12:25; 1 Corinthians 15:19

Bread: Job 13:15; Romans 5:3-5

Meal: Matthew 6:9-13

. . .

Lie: I can't make it through on earth with this trial. What if it never ends? This feels hopeless.

Truth: This will end; it's guaranteed when we see Jesus! So, we can have daily hope by His indwelling Spirit's filling work, as He sanctifies and strengthens us. We are constantly being carried by our sovereign and good God, our loving Father!

Milk: Psalm 33:18-22; Psalm 145:14; Romans 8:26-28

Bread: 2 Corinthians 4:16-17; 1 Peter 1:13

Meal: 1 Corinthians 15:50-55

My prayer to You, my God of living hope

In my suffering, You say this is true:

So, in my suffering, I praise You because:

In my suffering, please help me with:

Into my suffering, I'll sing these songs from my playlist today:

♪♪♪

Blessed assurance, Jesus is mine!
O what a foretaste of glory divine!
Heir of salvation, purchase of God,
born of his Spirit, washed in his blood.
Perfect submission, perfect delight,
visions of rapture now burst on my sight;
angels descending, bring from above
echoes of mercy, whispers of love.

Perfect submission, all is at rest;
I in my Savior am happy and blest;
watching and waiting, looking above,
filled with his goodness, lost in his love.
This is my story, this is my song,
praising my Savior all the day long;
this is my story, this is my song,
praising my Savior all the day long.

("BLESSED ASSURANCE," CROSBY, F., P. D.)

♪♪♪

11

HOW CAN I HANDLE MY EMOTIONS?

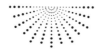

*C*hronic suffering often brings with it regular emotions that challenge us. Just like Job, we suffer physical, emotional, social, and financial loss. Job's story tells us that our emotions are part of the earthly human experience as we suffer. As we read his words of despair, like in chapters 3, 7, 10, 16, 17, and 30, we know deep emotional pain in suffering can be very real. So we need His help to walk *within* suffering on earth. How? Sometimes, we need professional help from trained Christian counselors. Sometimes we need medication and treatment for biological illnesses causing debilitating emotional responses.

But believers all need Scripture our great God has given to us. What are some emotional-cognitive ways His Word gives us to help us handle emotions as we suffer? He knows and understands, beloved, so He encourages us, "Don't lose heart...don't give up...don't be frightened... don't be dismayed." But how?

Job teaches us a unique way. We bring our emotions to God and listen to His voice of Scripture in call and response. "I lay my hand on my mouth" (40:4). Let's listen as we humbly hear God in His Word. We need to hear our Shepherd's voice speaking back to our cries. We must read or listen to the Bible daily and throughout the day as we walk through deep valleys. We come to Him with all of our needs, all of our questions, all of our emotions, and listen to His response. It's a posture of our heart that kneels before our Father of love, turns to our God of compassion and mercy with our pain, and continually seeks our sovereign, wise, good, and powerful God in the Bible. It's asking Him, "Search me, O God, and know my heart! Try me and know my thoughts! And see if there be any grievous way in me, and lead me in the way everlasting!" (Psalm 139:23-24). In Scripture, the Holy Spirit illuminates His voice speaking back to our hearts and turning them toward Him, over and over. And He knows exactly what we need to hear in His Word in every moment, to help us endure suffering.

In the Bible, we find many words of praise, awe, and worship to God tucked between the tears and fears of fellow sufferers. Praying these words from Scripture back to Him is His fantastic gift to help us endure profound suffering. As we do, we speak truth-full words to our hearts about who He is and what He's done for us. We praise Him for His promises and past, current, and forever grace as we read them. Then, we walk into these grace-filled truths, as He's strengthened us for the next hour.

So often, these truths prompt gratitude within us, stirring our emotions. For example, we read "the heavens declare the glory of God" (Psalm 19:1); then we only need to look outside and remember that God created and sustains and upholds the entire universe, including our lives! Words of praise bubble forth, even if our emotions are numb or sorrowful. And often? He brings a settled peace, even a quiet joy, amid our suffering and complex emotions.

～

List some truths you want to remember from the verses below.

Lie: I will never feel emotionally happy. It's never going to feel better. But I want to feel better.
Truth: We will feel forever happy when we live with Jesus one glorious day...so we can simply rest and abide with Jesus and His Word until that day.

Milk: Psalm 119:49-50, 81, 92, 107; John 17:25-26

Bread: John 15:1-11; Hebrews 4:12

Meal: 1 John 2:24-25

Lie: The worst is going to happen to me.
Truth: Even if the "worst" is death, we have hope that anything that happens is His loving best for us as He unfolds history toward the last day. And what will happen?

Milk: Luke 21:25-28; 2 Corinthians 4:16-18

Bread: 1 Corinthians 15:19-24

Meal: Psalm 139:16; Romans 8:35-39

Lie: Believers don't go through despair or depression.
Truth: Believers do...and God gives us many examples in His Word to comfort and encourage us, including Job.

Milk: Psalm 42; Psalm 126:5-6

Bread: Psalm 43; Psalm 116

Meal: 1 Kings 19:4-8; Psalm 34:18-19; Mark 14:34-36

My prayer to You, my God of abiding hope

In my suffering, You say this is true:

So, in my suffering, I praise You because:

In my suffering, please help me with:

Into my suffering, I'll sing these songs from my playlist today:

♪♪♪

Abide with me: fast falls the eventide:
the darkness deepens; Lord, with me abide:
when other helpers fail, and comforts flee,
help of the helpless, O abide with me.

Swift to its close ebbs out life's little day;
earth's joys grow dim, its glories pass away;
change and decay in all around I see;
O thou who changest not, abide with me.

I need thy presence every passing hour;
what but thy grace can foil the tempter's pow'r?
Who like thyself my guide and stay can be?
Through cloud and sunshine, O abide with me.

I fear no foe, with thee at hand to bless:
ills have no weight, and tears no bitterness.
Where is death's sting? where, grave, thy victory?
I triumph still, if thou abide with me.

Hold thou thy cross before my closing eyes:
shine through the gloom, and point me to the skies:
heav'n's morning breaks, and earth's vain shadows flee:
in life, in death, O Lord, abide with me.

("ABIDE WITH ME," LYTE, H. F., 1847)

♪♪♪

12

I NEED PEOPLE WHO UNDERSTAND ME BECAUSE IT SEEMS LIKE NO ONE GETS THIS

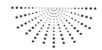

*J*ob's friends started well. They visited to "show him sympathy and comfort him" (2:11). They mourned with him; they wordlessly sat with him, "for they saw that his suffering was very great" (2:13). Maybe they didn't know what to say. Job himself was the first to speak, sharing his pain honestly...and then, their torrents of judgmental words began. Perhaps they thought they were "speaking the truth in love" (Ephesians 4:15), but God tells us they weren't speaking what "is right" about Him (42:7). They worsened Job's suffering through their presumptive, critical expressions of what they perceived of Job's heart, compounded by a wrongful understanding of God and the role of suffering in a believer's life. Some of what they shared were indeed Biblical truths, but those truths were tainted with lies. It made Job feel like "a byword of the peoples...one before whom men spit" (17:6), heightening his feelings of hopelessness. "Where then is my hope? Who will see my hope?" (17:15).

Beloved in Christ, many around us today react similarly and for the same reasons. So, suffering feels lonely and isolating. We ache for loved ones, friends, and professional caregivers to understand and offer comfort and hope, don't we? Yet, many don't do this well, so we feel unloved. I often wonder why we expect empathetic comfort. After all, humans are *all* sinners. Even believers, saved by grace, still have sin natures within. So sometimes, their words can hurt.

⁓

Perhaps, in those moments, Jesus gently calls to us, "Come to *me*, all who are weary and heavy-laden and I will give you rest" (Matthew 11:28). Our Comforter, the Spirit of Christ dwelling within us, knows our hearts, thoughts, emotions, griefs, and losses. Illuminating His Word to our hearts, He *perfectly* comforts us and gently convicts us of our sin, as those who no longer bear condemnation for our sin (John 3:16-17; Romans 8:1). In moments when we feel lonely, misunderstood, unloved, or even condemned by well-meaning others, He beckons us to the cross, where we find continual grace and perfect love.

I wonder if our desire for someone to "get this" is actually our longing for Jesus, our thirst for our true home, in which no sin exists. Our triune God understands...so our suffering can become a deepened time of intimate fellowship with Him, of abiding in Him, seeking to hear His voice speak back to our cries through His Word.

Perhaps, in our desperate desire for compassionate mercy from others, our suffering is something God is using to help us learn (and re-learn) forgiveness, to love our enemies, and to extend grace to those who do not offer it to us. Oh, this is so hard when we experience physical and emotional suffering! But by His Spirit's work, He helps us do this. For Jesus Himself continually wrestled with false accusations and abandonment of friends, as Job did. Jesus understands, and He empowers us by His Spirit.

What did our Friend, our Beloved Savior, pray as He suffered? "Father, forgive them, for they know not what they do" (Luke 23:34).

⁓

List some truths you want to remember from the verses below.

Lie: No one loves me, no one understands, and no one is my friend.
Truth: We are unified with Christ, with His continually present, comforting, compassionate, teaching, loving Spirit within us. What a friend we have in Jesus!

Milk: John 14:26; 1 Corinthians 3:16; Galatians 4:5-7

Bread: Romans 8:26-27; Ephesians 1:13

Meal: John 15:13; Ephesians 3:16-19

Lie: I should keep my feelings and thoughts to myself because someone might hurt or judge me.
Truth: Friends who offer gospel-centered truths of Scripture, who show the fruit of the Spirit, can be "safe" people, as we ask God for discernment.

Milk: Galatians 5:22-23

Bread: 1 Thessalonians 5:9-11; Isaiah 51:7

Meal: Proverbs 17:17; Colossians 3:12-14

Lie: No one can help me.

Truth: Suffering is a time of dependence on God, our Helper, for *all* our needs.

Milk: Isaiah 41:10; Hebrews 4:16, 13:6

Bread: John 14:26; 2 Corinthians 1:3-9

Meal: John 15:26

My prayer to You, my perfect Friend and Helper

In my suffering, You say this is true:

So, in my suffering, I praise You because:

In my suffering, please help me with:

Into my suffering, I'll sing these songs from my playlist today:

♪♪♪

Jesus! what a Friend for sinners!
Jesus! lover of my soul;
friends may fail me, foes assail me,
he, my Savior, makes me whole.

Jesus! what a strength in weakness!
Let me hide myself in him;
tempted, tried, and sometimes failing,
he, my strength, my victory wins.

Jesus! what a help in sorrow!
While the billows o'er me roll,
even when my heart is breaking,
he, my comfort, helps my soul.

Jesus! what a guide and keeper!
While the tempest still is high,
storms about me, night o'ertakes me,
he, my pilot, hears my cry.

Jesus! I do now receive him,
more than all in him I find;
he hath granted me forgiveness,
I am his, and he is mine.

Hallelujah! what a Savior!
Hallelujah, what a Friend!
Saving, helping, keeping, loving,
he is with me to the end.

("JESUS! WHAT A FRIEND FOR SINNERS!, CHAPMAN, J. W., 1910)

♪♪♪

13
THOUGHT-REPLACEMENT IN THE BATTLE

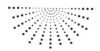

*J*n Job's lament, He continued to come to the Lord. In his honest agonies, he fought the accuser's lies spewed through his friends who "whitewash with lies; worthless physicians are you *all*" (13:4). He refused to give up hope in God entirely, despite having no evidence of his circumstances ever changing. When his friends urged him to repent of unconfessed sin, to manipulate God into fixing his circumstances, Job dug in hard to remind his heart of who God *is* and who Job is, as a believer. "Though he slay me, I will hope in him" (13:15).

By God's gracious gift, Job maintained hope in God, *into* His suffering. Although he heard nothing from God and only the words of his friends, he reminded himself of what he knew to be true about God. "But he knows the way that I take; when he has tried me, I shall come out as gold" (23:10). Into his physical pain and emotional groans, he interrupted and replaced lies in his thoughts with truths. "But he is unchangeable, and who can turn him back? What he desires, that he does. For he will complete what he appoints for me, and many such things are in his mind" (23:13-14).

~

A fourth friend, Elihu, begins talking toward the end of Job's story. God never rebukes Elihu but then begins to answer Job after Elihu's encouragement; we learn much from Elihu about what I call *thought replacement* as we suffer. Elihu urges Job to "take care; do not turn to iniquity" (36:21); "remember to extol his work, of which men have sung" (36:24); "keep listening to the thunder of his voice" (37:2); "stop and consider the wondrous works of God" (37:14). It's work in our minds...take care, remember, keep listening, stop, consider.

Elihu reminds us that we find hope in our suffering by actively replacing the same-old, tired lies of the devil with thankful truths about God's unchanging character. "He does great things that we cannot comprehend...whether for correction of for his land or for love, he causes it to happen...God is clothed with awesome majesty...he is great in power, justice and abundant righteousness he will not violate" (37:5, 13, 22-23).

~

On this side of the cross, we too find hope in our suffering by battling lies with *thought replacement*. But our thoughts are now as God's beloved and victorious children in Christ, in union with Jesus now and forever (Ephesians 1:19; Colossians 1:11; 2 Timothy 2:1)! So, we battle with the "strength of *his* might" (Ephesians 6:10, emphasis added), standing firm with gospel hope as those who have been given the "mind of Christ" (1 Corinthians 2:16).

It's hard work to maintain a Biblical perspective, and it's worth it! We battle as Jesus did when the devil tempted him, continually replacing lies with His Word, our offensive weapon (Ephesians 6:13-17). What a beautiful means of God's grace to us! What a gift to us when we feel so weak in the battles of suffering!

When the pain of suffering doesn't leave, we can then "boast all the more gladly" of our weaknesses because we remember that God says, "My grace is sufficient for you, for my power is made perfect in weakness" (2 Corinthians 12:9). We find hope, as we suffer, because Christ's divine power is within us, helping us to be content and strong in the sanctifying faith our suffering produces (2 Corinthians 12:10), as His indwelling Spirit makes us more like Jesus (2 Corinthians 3:18). All glory to our great God!

Let's hear the words of our Savior, praying for His disciples and us (John 17:20) as we battle lies with His thankful truths: "These things I speak in the world, that they may have my joy fulfilled in themselves. I do not ask that you take them out of the world, but that you keep them from the evil one. Sanctify them in the truth; your word is truth. I made known to them your name, and I will continue to make it known, that the love with which you have loved me may be in them, and I in them" (John 17:13, 15, 17, 26).

∾

List some thankful truths you want to remember as *thought replacements*, to battle the same-old, tired lies, from the verses below!

Psalm 23

Psalm 39:4-7

Matthew 24:6-8

John 11:25-26

Romans 5:8-11

Romans 6:19, 22

∾

Romans 8:9-10

Romans 8:23

Romans 8:28

Romans 8:31

Romans 8:38-39

Romans 16:20

~

1 Corinthians 1:30

2 Corinthians 4:7-10

2 Corinthians 4:16-18

2 Corinthians 5:21

Philippians 1:29

Philippians 2:5-11

Philippians 4:12-13

~

1 Thessalonians 4:13-18

2 Thessalonians 2:13

2 Timothy 1:9-11

Hebrews 2:14-15

Hebrews 9:14

Hebrews 13:20-21

~

James 1:12

1 Peter 1:2-6

1 Peter 1:7-9

1 John 3:23-24

My prayer to You, my Lord and Savior

In my suffering, You say this is true:

So, in my suffering, I praise You because:

In my suffering, please help me with:

Into my suffering, I'll sing these songs from my playlist today:

♪♪♪

Day by day and with each passing moment,
strength I find to meet my trials here;
trusting in my Father's wise bestowment,
I've no cause for worry or for fear.
He whose heart is kind beyond all measure
gives unto each day what he deems best—
lovingly, its part of pain and pleasure,
mingling toil with peace and rest.

Every day, the Lord himself is near me
with a special mercy for each hour;
all my cares he fain would bear, and cheer me,
he whose name is Counselor and Pow'r.
The protection of his child and treasure
is a charge that on himself he laid:
"As your days, your strength shall be in measure,"
this the pledge to me he made.

Help me then in every tribulation
so to trust your promises, O Lord,
that I lose not faith's sweet consolation
offered me within your holy Word.
Help me, Lord, when toil and trouble meeting,
e'er to take, as from a father's hand,
one by one, the days, the moments fleeting,
till I reach the promised land.

("Day by Day," Sandell, C., Skoog, A. L., trans., 1865)

♪♪♪

14

HOW CAN I POSSIBLY PRAISE
GOD RIGHT NOW?

*J*ob's cries are ours, in deep suffering. He sees troubled days ahead (14:1), with a self-focus on his pain and loss (14:22). He laments. Yet, into his cries, he stubbornly clings to glimmers of hope for something to come. "If a man dies, shall he live again? All the days of my service I would wait, till my renewal should come... my transgression would be sealed up in a bag, and you would cover over my iniquity" (14:14, 17). Do you see? Job is pointing us to Jesus, isn't he?

How can we possibly praise God right now? The same way Job did, interrupting his suffering with what I call *praise interruptions*. Using turnaround words like "but," "yet," or "therefore," we can cling to the sure hope of God's renewal, restoration, healing of sin, and all of its awful effects on our lives, in our forever-relationship with Him. We can praise Him because our Lord and Savior, Jesus Christ *has* covered over our iniquity. He "suffered once for sins, the righteous for the unrighteous, that he might bring us to God" (1 Peter 3:18).

～

Beloved in Christ, unlike Job, who had to look forward, we who belong to Christ now look backward to Jesus' death and resurrection. Jesus took all the punishment for our sin, gave us His righteousness instead, is alive and reigning over *all* things right now, dwells within us to carry us through any suffering we endure and is praying for us continually as He intercedes before our Father. Into our lament and sorrow, we can interrupt our pain by praising our beautiful Savior for who He is and what He's done for us. We can praise God for His gift of grace in making us His child and giving us faith in Christ.

Job had decided death was his only escape from suffering. Yes, death brings a believer home with the Lord. But, rather than looking for *escapes*, we can now *interrupt* our earthly suffering by praising Him for our eternal hope, especially as we wait for Him to return and restore all things to His sinless perfection in the new heaven and earth (Rev. 21).

I am suffering today, "*but* [my] citizenship is in heaven, and from it [I] await a Savior, the Lord Jesus Christ, who will transform [my] lowly body to be like his glorious body, by the power that enables him even to subject all things to himself" (Philippians 3:20-21). We can praise Him with hope for the end!

But we also have genuine hope as we endure suffering right now because God has given us this day with life and purpose, in union with Jesus. We're suffering, *but* "He has delivered us from the domain of darkness and transferred us to the kingdom of his beloved Son, in whom we have redemption, the forgiveness of sins" (Colossians 1:13-14). Today, we are living in union with the King of all...who is also our beloved Savior!

We can indeed praise Him into our suffering today, can't we?

We don't know what's next, around the corner in the earthly journey He's lovingly planned for us. Somehow, our suffering today is part of that journey and purpose, or He would have brought us home to Himself. So we can praise our good/loving/holy/wise/powerful God for giving us *Himself*, in a close relationship through Christ and with good purpose, as believers today. I'm suffering, and it hurts, "*but* he is unchangeable...he will complete what he appoints for me, and many such things are in his mind" (Job 23:13-14).

Job interrupted his suffering with *praise interruptions* like, "You have granted me life and steadfast love; and your care has preserved my spirit." (10:12). In Christ, we *have* a life now and forever, we *have* His unending and steadfast love, we *have* His continual care, and He *is* preserving our spirit, soul, and faith... until the day we see Him face to face! Job's *praise interruptions* pale compared to what our Lord promises to give us as we suffer in our time of history within His kingdom plan, as believers in Jesus Christ. And this? We can praise God for this...into today's suffering.

~

List some truths you want to remember from the verses below.

> **Lie:** I can praise You because I hope my suffering will end now.
> **Truth:** I can praise You because You are my living hope.

Milk: 1 Corinthians 15:19

Bread: Psalm 139; Romans 12:12

Meal: Ephesians 1:3-11; 1 Peter 4:19

Lie: I can praise You because I'm a good person with strength and faith.
Truth: By Your grace, I can praise You regardless of how good, strong, or faithful I feel.

Milk: Ephesians 2:8-10; 1 Peter 1:13

Bread: 2 Timothy 1:9-10

Meal: Ephesians 3:14-21

Lie: I can't praise You because my suffering is too intense.
Truth: As I lament my suffering, I can interrupt it by praising You with "turnaround" Scriptures, through Your Spirit.

Milk: Lamentations 3:17-26

Bread: 1 John 3:2-3

Meal: Psalm 89:1-18

**My prayer to You, my unchanging God of grace and beloved
Savior**

In my suffering, You say this is true:

So, in my suffering, I praise You because:

In my suffering, please help me with:

Into my suffering, I'll sing these songs from my playlist today:

♪♪♪

My Jesus, I love thee, I know thou art mine;
For thee all the follies of sin I resign.
My gracious Redeemer, my Saviour art thou;
If ever I loved thee, my Jesus, 'tis now.

I love thee because thou hast first loved me,
And purchased my pardon on Calvary's tree.
I love thee for wearing the thorns on thy brow;
If ever I loved thee, my Jesus, 'tis now.

I'll love thee in life, I will love thee in death;
And praise thee as long as thou lendest me breath;
And say, when the death-dew lies cold on my brow:
If ever I loved thee, my Jesus, 'tis now.

In mansions of glory and endless delight,
I'll ever adore thee in heaven so bright;
I'll sing with the glittering crown on my brow:
If ever I loved thee, my Jesus, 'tis now.

("MY JESUS, I LOVE THEE," FEATHERSTON, W. R., 1862)

♪♪♪

15

THE LORD IS THE SOURCE OF MY SONG!

*B*efore God Himself answered Job's cries, with majestic descriptions of His indescribable and grand character, Elihu serves as a warmup act. He reminds us that we naturally cry out for help from God (35:9). We sure do! And we must. But Elihu also condemns Job (and all of us) for the pride that so quickly bubbles to the surface as we suffer (35:12; 36:9).

Just as with Job, the enemy tries to make us pridefully forget who God is, so that our faith might waver when suffering lingers. We can think we know better than God, and we easily doubt. Elihu helps us! He reminds Job and us that "God is greater than man" (33:12), that He would never do anything wicked, evil, or wrong (34:10-12), that He is in charge of the entire universe and our very breath (34:13-15), that He sees and knows everything (34:21), that He is "mighty in strength of understanding" (36:5), and that "He is great in power; justice and abundant righteousness he will not violate" (37:23). This is our God. "He does great things that we cannot comprehend" (37:5).

But Elihu also reminds us that, in our suffering, God is teaching us something (35:11). He "opens our ears to instruction...by adversity" (36:10, 15). In this way, "he *delivers* the afflicted *by* their affliction" (36:15, emphasis added). Consider our beloved Savior and Deliverer, always a patient teacher. Remember Jesus, a teacher who humbly washed the feet of His students before He suffered all the punishment they deserved. Jesus is also our tender teacher, holy in wisdom, goodness, and love, who lives within us as we suffer. Elihu points forward to Jesus as he reminds us of our hope: "He has redeemed my soul from going down into the pit, and my life shall look upon the light" (33:28).

In Jesus, we know God's gracious and loving gift of salvation and enduring faith, all the way to the end. In Jesus, we know He's coming alongside us to teach us something for His "best-good-for-us" as we suffer. In Jesus, we know that our earthly lives are meant to bring Him glory. Our teacher-guide knows precisely what we need for all of it, by His grace, for our good, and His glory.

God also knows we need our "Maker, who *gives* songs in the night" (Job 35:10, emphasis added). He knows we *need* to praise Him because we need hope as we suffer. It's how He made us. "Why are you cast down, O my soul, and why are you in turmoil within me? Hope in God, for I shall again praise him, my salvation and my God" (Psalm 42:5). Throughout Scripture, God extols us to praise Him, to sing praise to Him because He is worthy of our praise. In suffering? Yes, it's not only possible and commanded by our loving Father, but it helps us endure. He gives us hope as we do, helping us find hope in suffering, singing of our *hope in Him.*

"By day the LORD commands his steadfast love, and at night his song is with me, a prayer to the God of my life" (Ps. 42:8).

This can only be by His Spirit's work, for these are tender times in which we are humbled, in which He draws us toward awe and worship of our living God, our steadfastly loving Lord of life. These are times when we fall before Him in our need, asking Him to help us praise Him for what is true, as He helps us get through the next hour of suffering. These are times when He teaches us more of His comfort, His strength, and His love...giving Himself in His Word.

The Lord Himself is the source of our song.

So, let's interrupt our suffering as we sing of our gospel hope daily. Let's praise God for who He is and what He's done for us in Jesus Christ, finding hope in Him, into our suffering.

∼

List some truths you want to remember from the verses below.

Lie: I know what is best for my life.
Truth: My loving God knows what is best for my life, and He graciously gives me all things I need, continually.

Milk: Matthew 11:29; Romans 8:31-34

Bread: Psalm 77:6; Romans 8:28-30

Meal: Romans 8:35-39

Lie: If I'm suffering, I can't experience anything positive.
Truth: By His Spirit's filling, God promises to give us so much good as we suffer.

Milk: John 16:33; Philippians 4:11-12; Romans 15:13

Bread: Psalm 149:5; Romans 5:1-5; Philippians 4:13

Meal: Isaiah 54:10; 1 John 4:4; Habakkuk 3:17-19

Lie: Other than relief from suffering in the end, there is no reward for this awful pain.
Truth: God gives His abundant rewards to believers as they walk through suffering on earth.

Milk: Philippians 1:6, 3:10-11, 14

Bread: Romans 8:18; 1 Corinthians 2:9

Meal: James 1:12; Matthew 25:21

My prayer to You, my Teacher, my God, my song in the night

In my suffering, You say this is true:

So, in my suffering, I praise You because:

In my suffering, please help me with:

Into my suffering, I'll sing these songs from my playlist today:

♪♪♪

Come, thou Almighty King,
help us thy name to sing, help us to praise.
Father, all glorious, o'er all victorious,
come and reign over us,
Ancient of Days.

Come, thou Incarnate Word,
gird on thy mighty sword, our prayer attend.
Come, and thy people bless,
and give thy Word success;
Spirit of holiness, on us descend.

Come, Holy Comforter,
thy sacred witness bear in this glad hour.
Thou who almighty art,
now rule in every heart,
and ne'er from us depart,
Spirit of pow'r.

To the great One in Three eternal praises be,
hence evermore.
His sovereign majesty may we in glory see,
and to eternity
love and adore.

("COME, THOU ALMIGHTY KING," SOURCE UNKNOWN, C. 1757)

Praise God, from whom all blessings flow;
Praise Him, all creatures here below;
Praise Him above, ye heav'nly host;
Praise Father, Son, and Holy Ghost.
Amen.

("DOXOLOGY," KEN, T., 1709)

♪♪♪

HELPFUL RESOURCES FOR A
CHRISTIAN WALKING THROUGH
SUFFERING

Alcorn, R. (2009). *If God is good: Faith in the midst of suffering and evil.* Multnomah.

Ash, C. (2014). *Job: The wisdom of the cross.* Crossway.

Ash, C. (2021). *Trusting God in the darkness: A guide to understanding the book of Job.* Crossway.

Bridges, J. (2016). *Trusting God.* NavPress.

Christensen, S. (2020). *What about evil?: A defense of God's sovereign glory.* P & R.

Elliot, E. (2019). *Suffering is never for nothing.* B & H Books.

Guthrie, N. (2006). *Holding onto hope: A pathway through suffering to the heart of God.* Tyndale Momentum.

Keller, T. (2015). *Walking with God through pain and suffering.* Penguin.

Ortlund, D. (2020). *Gentle and lowly: The heart of Christ for sinners and sufferers.* Crossway.

Ortlund, E. (2021). *Piercing Leviathan: God's defeat of evil in the book of Job (New studies in Biblical theology 56).* IVP Academic.

Sproul. R. C. (2009). *Surprised by suffering.* Ligonier.

Story, L. (2015). *When God doesn't fix it: Lessons you never wanted to learn, truths you can't live without.* Thomas Nelson.

Tada, J. E., & Estes, S. (2000). *When God weeps: Why our sufferings matter to the Almighty.* Zondervan.

Tada, J. E. (2015). *A place of healing: Wrestling with the mysteries of suffering, pain, and God's sovereignty.* David C. Cook.

Tripp, P. D. (2018). *Suffering: Gospel hope when life doesn't make sense.* Crossway.

Turnage, E. (2019). *The waiting room: 60 meditations for finding peace and hope in a health crisis.* Living Story.

SOME AFTERTHOUGHTS

First, thank you so much for reading this book. I've prayed it would be the Lord's blessing as you walk through this difficult time.

As you may know, many people read **Amazon reviews** before deciding to read a book. Could you please take a minute to review this book and share some honest feedback with me and others? It would help me in creating future projects. Simple star reviews will also help other sufferers find the book.

Second, I am creating **weekly playlist gifts** of Psalms, hymns, and spiritual songs to coordinate with each chapter. They're for our use in personal worship time as praise-filled prayer responses to the Lord. Contact me at laurihogle.com if you would like to receive them in your email each week.

Third, this is my most profound **prayer for you**, fellow sufferer. "May the God of hope fill you with all joy and peace in believing, so that by the power of the Holy Spirit you may abound in hope" (Romans 15:13).

In Christ,
Lauri

NOTES

"THIS IS MY STORY, THIS IS MY SONG!"

1. Taken from *My Utmost for His Highest*® by Oswald Chambers, © 1935 by Dodd Mead & Co., renewed © 1963 by the Oswald Chambers Publications Assn., Ltd. Used by permission of Our Daily Bread Publishing, Grand Rapids, MI 49501. All rights reserved.
2. Copyright © 1971 HannaStreet Music (BMI) (adm. at CapitolCMGPublishing.com) All rights reserved. Used by permission.
3. Spurgeon, C. (1866). *Morning & Evening*, August 18.

ACKNOWLEDGMENTS

As J. S. Bach inscribed on his notated manuscripts, I praise the Lord with "Soli Deo Gloria." It is for God's glory that this book exists, by His amazing grace.

I am forever thankful to my dear husband Paul for his encouragement and support. It has been for better, for worse, for richer, for poorer, in sickness and in health, until death do us part. I love you.

I'm so grateful to my children, extended family, church friends, readers who have become new friends, and sister authors who have shone the light of Jesus into the darkness and prayed for me and this book.

To the many pastors and Bible teachers who have been God's gift of grace to me, thank you.

One day, I will thank the hymn writers! I praise God for the hymns and songs that have been His gifts of grace to my suffering mind, heart, and body.

Because this particular book is so steeped in some of the hardest theological concepts, I was deeply concerned about "rightly handling the word of truth" (2 Tim. 2:15). With profound gratitude, I thank the pastors who graciously took the time to review the draft manuscript, "check my work," and offer comments and wisdom to me: Rev. Jeremy Byrd, Rev. Daniel Millward, Rev. Silas Santos, and Pastors Larry Brodie and Dan Southam. Your encouragement was the Lord's "couraging into" me as I wrote of these difficult topics. Thank you.

"To the only wise God be glory forevermore through Jesus Christ! Amen" (Rom. 16:27).

SDG

ABOUT THE AUTHOR

Dr. Lauri Hogle's journey of suffering interweaves with her lifelong passion for glorifying God through music, teaching, research, and writing. As a church music/children's/women's ministry leader, music educator, music therapist, research scholar, and author, her words and musical offerings have touched lives across the globe. She is the founder of Singing Christ's Hope, a nonprofit ministry for Christian women walking through suffering. Although she has been a prolific academic writer, active speaker, and teacher, her greatest joy is as a wife, mother, and Nana. God's sweet gifts of grace include continual stacks of books, coffee, knitting, candles, and beautiful foretastes of eternal song.

You can find and contact Lauri at www.laurihogle.com.

ALSO BY LAURI A. HOGLE, PHD

Near to God: A Devotional Bible Study of God's Character in Our Suffering

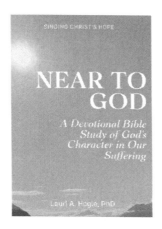

Some comments from readers:

"Such an amazing book to help in healing."

"My heart always wanders to focus on self, especially in the midst of fiery trials. What a treasure to have a tool like this that plucks me out of the ash heap of my own misery and sets me on high places, worshipping my great God!"

"Such an encouraging book—true comfort and hope"

"The author points to Scriptures that will engage your heart and mind; and will lead you into fruitful times of worshipping in spirit and truth, finding true comfort and being able to exult in His mercies, His love, and our true hope."

"The devotionals are God-focused instead of focused on looking inward."

"This devotional book is a close friend to any who are suffering."

"A simple devotional length with rich treasures to find each day. Wrapping each day up with songs of worship."

"A must-have."

Praying God's Promises Into Suffering: A Devotional Bible Study Prayer Journal

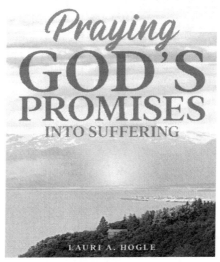

A Devotional Bible
Study Prayer Journal

Praying
GOD'S
PROMISES
INTO SUFFERING

LAURI A. HOGLE

Some words from readers:

"I know Lauri personally. She is sweet and gentle even as she is going through tremendous pain and a multitude of other symptoms. This book will touch your heart. She provides prompts for you to evaluate your own heart in regard to your thoughts and feelings about what you're going through in relation to God. Beautifully done."

"This simple and short devotional is packed with hymns of the faith and the unchanging faithfulness of God in all our circumstances. As a person who suffers with chronic pain and panic attacks, this book has been a lifesaver for me. Lauri lays out God's promises that never change and how we need to focus, cling, and stand in faith no matter what suffering we go through. I highly recommend this for anyone whether suffering with loss, physical, mental or spiritual battles that we can face on a daily basis. God promises never to leave us or forsake us and this book is a helpful guide and journal to pray God's promises to us."

"This book is written by someone who understands suffering and she encourages us who suffer chronic pain and illness to continue to trust in the Lord through it all. This book teaches me to turn Bible verses and songs into prayers, as I suffer."

BONUS!

If you would like weekly personal prayers and professionally curated Christian music playlists to accompany these Bible study devotional prayer journals, sign up at laurihogle.com and they will come to your email. You can sing the gospel to yourself as you pray-sing to our God!

Made in the USA
Columbia, SC
07 February 2024

31645583R00072